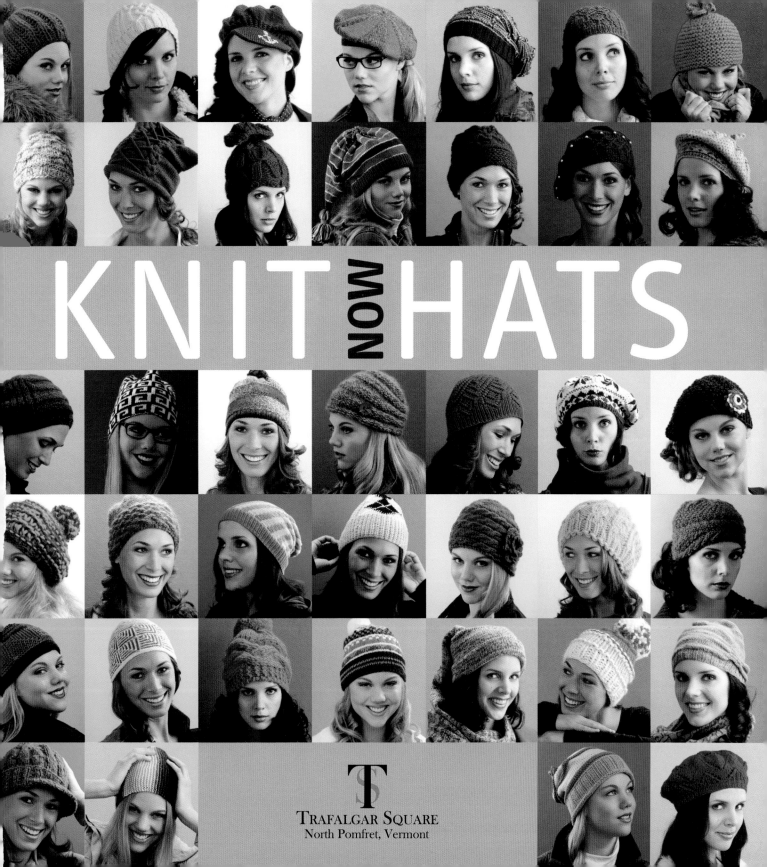

KNIT NOW HATS

T
TRAFALGAR SQUARE
North Pomfret, Vermont

First published in the United States of America in 2013 by
Trafalgar Square Books
North Pomfret, Vermont 05053
www.trafalgarbooks.com

Originally published in German as Kopfsache: Mützen Stricken
Copyright © 2012 frechverlag GmbH, 70499 Stuttgart, Germany (www.frechverlag.de)
English language translation © 2013 Trafalgar Square Books

This edition is published by arrangement with Claudia Böhme Rights & Literary Agency, Hannover, Germany (www.agency-boehme.com).

ISBN: 978-1-57076-641-1

Library of Congress Control Number: 2013937970

Project Management: Miriam Heil
Editor: Andrea Müh and Miriam Heil
Translator: Donna Druchunas
Hair and Makeup: Diekmann face art, Ludwigsburg
Layout: Petra Theilfarth
Photography: Frechverlag GmbH, 70499 Stuttgart; Lichtpunkt, Michael Ruder, Stuttgart

Printed in China

10 9 8 7 6 5 4 3 2 1

Foreword

What you wear defines your style, providing a visual outlet for your personality. And what's easier to wear than a great-looking hat? Hats are the perfect accessory for adding a touch of class, a little spice, or a splash of color to an outfit. Plus, they are the perfect small knitting project: inexpensive to make and portable, so you can always have one in your bag when you're on the go. They're quick to finish, too, so you can try out tons of creative ideas!

Find the right one—or several!

Colors [DESIGNED BY FRAUKE KIEDAISCH]

LEVEL OF DIFFICULTY
 Easy

SIZE
Circumference 21¼-22¾ in / 54-58 cm

MATERIALS
Yarn: (CYCA #6), Lana Grossa Ragazza Lei (100% Merino; 43 yd/39 m / 50 g), Pink 15, 100 g and Red 33, 50 g

Needles: U.S. size 15 / 10 mm: set of 5 dpn and 24 in / 60 cm circular

Stitch markers

GAUGE
8 sts and 22 rnds in Brioche stitch = 4 x 4 in / 10 x 10 cm.

Adjust needle size to obtain correct gauge if necessary.

PATTERN STITCHES
Ribbing
All rnds: (P1, k1) around.

Brioche Stitch
Work in 32-rnd stripe pattern: 8 rnds in Red, 10 rnds in Pink, 8 rnds in Red, 6 rnds in Pink.
Rnd 1: (P1, k1) around.
Rnd 2: (P1, sl 1 pw, yo) around.
Rnd 3: (Sl 1 pw, yo, knit the next st tog with the yo) around.
Rnd 4: (Knit the next st tog with the yo, sl 1 pw, yo) around
Rep Rnds 3 and 4.

INSTRUCTIONS
With Pink, CO 40 sts. Divide sts evenly on 4 dpn (10 sts per needle), and join to work in the round, being careful not to twist sts.
Work 4 rnds in ribbing, beg the rnd with a purl.
Begin working in Brioche stitch, changing colors as indicated for 32-rnd stripe pattern.

CROWN SHAPING
Rnd 1: With Pink (p1, knit the next st tog with the yo) around.
Rnd 2: K2tog around—20 sts rem, 5 on each ndl.
Rnd 3: Knit.
Rnd 4: K2tog around—10 sts rem.

FINISHING
Run the tail of yarn through the rem 10 sts and tighten to fasten off. Weave in ends. With Pink, make a 4 in / 10 cm pompom (see page 95), and attach securely to the top of the hat.

Pure Nature [DESIGNED BY HEIKE ROLAND]

SIZE

Circumference 20½-22 in / 52-56 cm

MATERIALS

Yarn: (CYCA #4), Lana Grossa Alta Moda Alpaca (90% alpaca, 5% virgin wool, 5% polyamide; 153 yd/140 m / 50 g), Natural 014, 100 g

Needles: U.S. size 8 / 5 mm: set of 5 dpn

Cable needle

GAUGE

17 sts and 22 rows in St st = 4 x 4 in / 10 x 10 cm.

Adjust needle size to obtain correct gauge if necessary.

CHART

Page 91

PATTERN STITCHES

Ribbing

All rnds: (K2, p2) around.

Cable Pattern

Even-numbered rnds are not shown on chart until row 36. On even Rnds 2-34, knit the knits and purl the purls. Work Rnds 1-35 of chart for body of hat. Beginning with Rnd 36, all rows are charted. Beg decreasing for crown as charted with Rnd 36. Work 66-st repeat twice around hat and work Rnds 1-53 of chart once.

INSTRUCTIONS

CO 132 sts. Divide sts on 4 dpns (34 sts on ndls 1 and 3 and 32 sts on ndls 2 and 4). Join to work in the rnd, being careful not to twist sts.

Work 10 rnds of ribbing.

Work cable pattern, following chart through Rnd 53—40 sts rem.

FINISHING

Run the tail of yarn through the rem sts and tighten to fasten off. Weave in ends.

Wanderlust  [DESIGNED BY LYDIA KLÖS]

LEVEL OF DIFFICULTY
Intermediate

SIZE
Circumference 22-22¾ in / 56-58 cm

MATERIALS
Yarn: (CYCA #3), Schachenmayr SMC Extra Merino (100% Merino; 142 yd/130 m / 50 g), Navy Blue 50, 100 g

Needles: U.S. size 2-3 / 3 mm: 7 dpn

Notions: Seed beads: 4 mm pearl white, 2.6 mm yellow

Blue sewing thread

Beading needle

Foam rubber sheet in blue, approx. 8 x 12 in / 20 cm x 30 cm, 1/16 in / 2 mm thick

GAUGE
24 sts and 33 rows in St st = 4 x 4 in / 10 x 10 cm.

Adjust needle size to obtain correct gauge if necessary

BRIM TEMPLATE
page 90

BEADING CHART
page 91

PATTERN STITCHES
Ribbing (Multiple of 3)
Rnd 1: (K2, p1) around.
Rnd 2: *Work 2-st right cross (first knit the 2nd st, then knit the 1st st), p1; rep from * around.
Rep Rnds 1-2 for pattern.

Stockinette Stitch (St st)
Back and forth: Knit RS rows and purl WS rows.
In the round: Knit all rnds.

Short Rows
Row 1 (RS): Knit to the last 2 sts. Do not work these sts. Turn.
Row 2 (WS): Yo, purl to the last 2 sts. Do not work these sts. Turn.
Row 3: Yo, knit to the last 3 sts. Do not work these sts. Turn.
Row 4: Yo, purl to the last 3 sts. Do not work these sts. Turn.
Rows 5-20: Rep Rows 3 and 4 leaving 1 more stitch unworked at the end of each row

Anchor Motif
Working back and forth in St st, place beads (see page 94) as shown on the chart.
Work Rows 1-16 of chart once.

INSTRUCTIONS
CO 111 sts. Divide sts over 6 dpn (5 ndls with 18 sts each, 1 ndl with 21 sts). Join to work in the rnd, being careful not to twist sts.
Work 7 rnds in ribbing.
Change to St st and on the first rnd, inc 66 sts as foll: *K2, M1, k2, M1, k1, M1; rep from * around, ending with k1—177 sts.
On the second rnd, end every second ndl with M1 and divide sts evenly over 6 ndls—180 sts.
Work even in St st until piece measures 4 in / 10 cm from ribbing.

CROWN SHAPING
To shape crown, continue in St st and on the next rnd, k2tog at beg and end of each ndl—12 sts decreased. Dec the same way on every other rnd until 1 st rem on each ndl—6 sts.
Run the tail of yarn through the rem sts and tighten to fasten off. Weave in ends.

BRIM
With the end of rnd at the center back of the hat and RS facing, pick up and knit 47 sts along the CO edge at center front.
Work back and forth on 2 ndls in St st with short rows, centering Anchor motif on brim. After the 20th short row, work a yo at the beg of the next WS row, then purl across all sts, purling each yo tog with the following st.
Then, repeat short rows, working in reverse, stopping the first row 11 sts before the end. Work one more stitch in each row. When all sts have been worked, work a yo at the beg of the next WS row, then purl across all sts, purling each yo tog with the following st.
BO, leaving a tail approx. 19¾ in / 50 cm long.

FINISHING
Using the pattern for the brim template, trace the shape onto the foam and cut out. Insert into the brim and sew the opening closed. Sew on the anchor chain with yellow beads.

Amour [DESIGNED BY ANJA BELLE]

LEVEL OF DIFFICULTY

 Intermediate

SIZE

Circumference 21¼-22 in / 54-56 cm

MATERIALS

Yarn: (CYCA #2), Schoppel-Wolle Zauberwolle (100% Merino; 273 yd /250 m / 100 g), Toasted Almond 1874 and Stonewashed 1535, 100 g each

Needles: U.S. size 1-2 / 2.5 mm: set of 5 dpn; U.S. size 2-3 / 3 mm: set of 5 dpn and 24 in / 60 cm circular

GAUGE

20 sts and 29 rows in St st using larger needles = 4 x 4 in / 10 x 10 cm.

Adjust needle sizes to obtain correct gauge if necessary.

TECHNIQUES

Double Knitting

In double knitting, 2 stitches knit in different colors form 1 stitch pair. The resulting fabric is double-thick and each side is a different color. To create each double stitch, knit into the next stitch using the first color (this will be a knit st in following rnds), then knit into the back of the same stitch using the second color (this will be a purl st in following rnds). On subsequent rnds, the first st of each pair is knit and is shown on the RS of the work; the second st of each pair is purled and will fall on the WS of the work. Make sure to move both yarns to the front or back of the needle when knitting and purling so all of the yarn strands fall between the two layers of knitting.

Increasing in Double Knitting

Lift the bars of both colors of yarn between the stitches onto the left needle. Knit the first stitch with the front color and purl the second st through the back with the second color.

Decreasing in Double Knitting

Slip the first st of the next pair to the right needle, then swap the position of the next 2 sts on the left needle. Put the first st back onto the left needle. You now have 2 stitch pairs with 2 stitches of the same color next to each other. Knit the first 2 sts tog and purl the second 2 sts tog.

PATTERN STITCHES

Stockinette Stitch (St st)
All rnds: Knit.

Ribbing
All rnds: (K1, p1) around.

INSTRUCTIONS

With Stonewashed and larger needles, CO 4 sts. Divide onto dpn and join to work in the rnd, being careful not to twist sts.

Rnd 1: Kf&b around—8 sts.

Rnd 2: (K1, kf&b) around—12 sts.

Rnd 3: Kf&b around—24 sts.

Rnd 4: Join Toasted Almond, *(in the next st k with Stonewashed and ktbl with Toasted Almond) twice, then (in the next st, k with Toasted Almond and ktbl with Stonewashed twice); rep from * around—24 st pairs.

Double Knit Crown

As you work in double knitting, each stitch will always be worked in the same color as stitch below.

Rnd 5: Work even in Double Knitting as set.

Rnd 6: (Work 1 st pair, inc 1 pair, work 1 st pair) 12 times—12 sts increased.

Rnds 7 and 8: Work even in Double Knitting as set.

Rnd 9: (Work 1 st pair, inc 1 pair, work 2 sts pairs) 12 times—12 sts increased.

Rep Rnds 7-9, increasing every 3rd rnd with one more st pair worked after each increase pair until the hat measures 10¼ in / 26 cm across.

Begin dec every 3rd rnd, working the second and third stitch pairs in each color segment as Double Knitted Decreases until hat opening measures 6 in / 15.5 cm across.

Brim

Cut Toasted Almond and continue working in Stonewashed. Change to smaller needles. K2tog-tbl around, turning each st pair into a single st. Work in k1, p1 ribbing for 2 in / 5 cm. BO all sts.

FINISHING

Weave in ends.

In Profile [DESIGNED BY JUTTA BÜCKER]

LEVEL OF DIFFICULTY

 Easy

SIZE

Circumference 19¾-21¼ in / 50-54 cm

MATERIALS

Yarn: (CYCA #4), Zitron Zeitlos (100% Merino; 262 yd/240 m / 100 g), Black 130 and Grey Heather 03, 100 g each

Needles: U.S. size 7 / 4.5 mm: set of 5 dpn or 16 in / 40 cm circular

GAUGE

24 sts and 30 rows in Ribbing = 4 x 4 in / 10 x 10 cm.

19 sts and 40 rows in Structured Stripe Pattern = 4 x 4 in / 10 x 10 cm.

Adjust needle size to obtain correct gauge if necessary.

PATTERN STITCHES

Ribbing
All rnds: (K2, p2) around.

Stockinette Stitch (St st)
All rnds: Knit.

Reverse Stockinette Stitch (rev St st)
All rnds: Purl.

STRUCTURED STRIPE PATTERN

(Multiple of 10)
Rnds 1-4: Knit.
Rnd 5: (P5, yo, k1, yo, p4) around.
Rnds 6-7: (P5, k3, p4) around.
Rnd 8: (P5, k3tog, p4) around.
Rep Rnds 1-8 for pattern.

INSTRUCTIONS

With Black, CO 108 sts. Join to work in the rnd, being careful not to twist sts. Work in ribbing for 2 in / 5 cm. Change to Grey Heather and Structured Stripe Pattern, increasing 2 sts in 1st rnd—110 sts.
Work Rnds 1-8 of Structured Stripe Pattern 11 times (approx. 8¼ in / 21 cm)
Change to Black and work in St st for 1½ in / 4 cm.

FINISHING

Cut yarn leaving a long tail. Run the tail of yarn through all of the sts and tighten to fasten off. Weave in ends.

Mischief [DESIGNED BY MONIKA ECKERT]

LEVEL OF DIFFICULTY

Experienced

SIZE

Circumference 22-22¾ in / 56-58 cm

MATERIALS

Yarn: (CYCA #2), Zitron Unisono (100% Merino; 328 yd/300 m / 100 g), Purple 1162, 100 g

Needles: U.S. size 4 / 3.5 mm: set of 5 dpn and 2 circulars 24 in / 60 cm

Cable needle or extra dpn

GAUGE

23 sts and 40 rows in Lozenge pattern = 4 x 4 in / 10 x 10 cm.

Adjust needle size to obtain correct gauge if necessary.

CHART

Lozenge Pattern

Work as charted. Only odd-numbered rnds are shown. On even rounds, knit the knits and yarnovers, and purl the purls. The repeat is worked 4 times around the hat. Rnds 1-74 are worked once.

Repeat = 27 sts after Rnd 23

■ = knit

− = purl

○ = yo

◢ = k2tog

∩ = CDD (sl 2tog kw, k1, p2sso)

＋ = M1

≪ = ssk (Sl 1-kw twice, insert the left ndl into the front of the 2 slipped sts and k2tog-tbl)

▲ = k3tog

△ = sl 1, k2tog, psso

= sl 2 to cn and hold in front, k2, k2 from cn

INSTRUCTIONS

With dpn or 2 circs, CO 8 sts. Divide sts evenly on dpn or circulars; join to work in the rnd, being careful not to twist st. Knit 1 rnd.

In the next rnd, kf&b around—16 sts.

Knit 1 rnd, then begin Lozenge pattern, working the chart 4 times around.

When you have enough sts, switch to working on 1 circular ndl; pm at beg of rnd.

When all charted rows are complete, BO all sts loosely. Draw end through rem sts and tighten.

FINISHING

Weave in ends.

Water Play [DESIGNED BY HELGA SPITZ]

LEVEL OF DIFFICULTY

 Easy

SIZE

Circumference 21¼ -22 in / 54-56 cm

MATERIALS

Yarn: (CYCA #6), Lana Grossa Ragazza Lei
(100% Merino; 43 yd/39 m / 50 g), Turquoise
28, 100 g

Needles: U.S. size 13 / 9 mm: set of 5 dpn

Crochet hook: U.S. size L or M/N / 8 or 9 mm

GAUGE

9 sts and 18 rows in garter stitch = 4 x 4 in /
10 x 10 cm.

Adjust needle size to obtain correct gauge if
necessary.

PATTERN STITCHES

Garter Stitch

Rnd 1: Knit.

Rnd 2: Purl.

Rep Rnds 1-2 for pattern.

INSTRUCTIONS

CO 54 sts. Divide sts onto dpn and join to work in
the rnd, being careful not to twist sts.

Work around in Garter st until hat measures 7 in /
18 cm, ending with a purl rnd.

Crown Shaping

Next rnd: (K1, k2tog) 18 times—36 sts rem.

Without decreasing, purl 1 rnd, knit 1 rnd,
purl 1 rnd.

Next rnd: K2tog around—18 sts rem.

Purl 1 rnd.

Next rnd: K2tog around until 8 sts rem.

FINISHING

Run the tail of yarn through rem sts and tighten
to fasten off. Weave in ends.

POMPOM

With crochet hook, *ch 15, 1 sc at the center of the
hat; rep from * 12 times. Fasten off.

Fashionista [DESIGNED BY TANJA STEINBACH]

LEVEL OF DIFFICULTY
 Intermediate

SIZE
Circumference 21¼-22 in / 54-56 cm

MATERIALS
YARN FOR BEIGE HAT
(CYCA #6), Schachenmayr/SMC Elements Mix (55% acrylic, 18% polyamide, 10% wool, 6% mohair; 33 yd/30 m / 50 g) in Sahara Color 80, 100 g

(CYCA #6), Schachenmayr/SMC Boston (70 % acrylic, 30% wool; 60 yd/55 m / 50 g), Sisal 04, 50 g

YARN FOR RED HAT
(CYCA #6), Schachenmayr/SMC Elements Mix (55% acrylic, 18% polyamide, 10% wool, 6% mohair; 33 yd/30 m / 50 g) in Esprit Color 82, 100 g

(CYCA #6), Schachenmayr/SMC Boston (70% acrylic, 30% wool; 60 yd/55 m / 50 g), Burgundy 31, 50 g

Needles: U.S. size 11 / 7 or 8 mm: set of 5 dpn and 16 in / 40 cm circular

Stitch markers

Fur pompom with snap in matching color

GAUGE
12-13 sts and 24-25 rnds in Slip Stitch Pattern = 4 x 4 in / 10 x 10 cm.

Adjust needle size to obtain correct gauge if necessary.

PATTERN STITCHES
Stockinette Stitch (St st)
All rnds: Knit.

Reverse Stockinette Stitch (rev St st)
All rnds: Purl.

Ribbing
All rnds: (K2, p2) around

Note: Slip sts pw wyib.

INSTRUCTIONS
With Sahara Color/Esprit Color, CO 48 sts. Divide sts evenly on 4 dpn and join to work in the round, being careful not to twist sts.

Work in ribbing for 1½ in / 4 cm.

Rnd 1: Change to Sisal/ Burgundy and inc 16 sts: (K3, M1) around—64 sts total.

If sts no longer fit on dpn, change to circular needle and add marker for beg of rnd.

Begin Slip Stitch Pattern as follows:

Rnds 2 and 3: With Sisal/Burgundy, purl.

Rnds 4-9: With Sahara Color/Esprit Color, (k2, sl 2, k4) around.

Rnd 10: With Sisal/Burgundy, knit.

Rnds 11 and 12: Rep Rnds 2 and 3.

Rnds 13-18: With Sahara Color/Esprit Color, (k6, sl 2) around.

Rnds 19-21: With Sisal/Burgundy, work as for Rnds 10-12.

Rnds 22-27: With Sahara Color/Esprit color, work as for Rnds 4-9.

Rnds 28-30: With Sisal/Burgundy, work as for Rnds 10-12.

CROWN SHAPING
Hat measures approx. 6¼ in / 16 cm from ribbing.

Rnd 31: With Sahara Color/Esprit Color, *(K1, k2tog) twice, sl 2; rep from * around—48 sts rem.

Rnds 32-36: With Sahara Color/Esprit Color, (k4, sl 2) around.

Rnds 37-39: With Sisal/Burgundy, work as for Rnds 10-12.

Rnd 40: With Sahara Color/Esprit Color, *K1, sl 1, (k2tog) twice; rep from * around—32 sts rem.

Rnds 41-43: With Sahara Color/Esprit Color, (k1, sl 1, k2) around.

Rnd 44: With Sisal/Burgundy, knit.

Rnd 45: With Sisal/Burgundy, p2tog around—16 sts rem.

Rnd 46: With Sisal/Burgundy, k2tog around—8 sts rem.

FINISHING
Run the tail of yarn through rem sts twice and tighten to fasten off. Weave in ends.
Sew snap to top of hat.
Sew other side of snap to pompom if it is not already attached.

Note: Instead of a fur pompom, you can use the Boston yarn to make a pompom approx. 3 in / 7-8 cm in diameter (see page 95) and sew it to the top of the hat.

Vintage Lace-up [DESIGNED BY NADJA BRANDT]

LEVEL OF DIFFICULTY

 Intermediate

SIZE

Circumference 20½-22 in / 52-56 cm

MATERIALS

Yarn: (CYCA #1), Regia Extra Twist Merino (75% Merino, 25% polyamide; 230 yd/210 m / 50 g), Petrol 9357, 150 g

Needles: U.S. sizes 3 and 4 / 3.25 and 3.5 mm: sets of 5 dpn

Stitch markers

2 short dpn U.S. size 2-3 / 2.5 mm

Large-eye darning needle

GAUGE

21 sts and 30 rows in St st using smaller needles = 4 x 4 in / 10 x 10 cm.

Adjust needle sizes to obtain correct gauge if necessary.

PATTERN STITCHES

Stockinette Stitch (St st)
All rnds: Knit.

Cable
(Multiple of 10)
Sl 2 sts to cn and hold in back, k3, k2 from cn; then sl 3 sts to cn and hold in front, k2, k3 from cn.

Note: The entire hat is knit with 2 strands of yarn held together.

INSTRUCTIONS

With 2 strands of yarn held tog and smaller needles, loosely CO 120 sts. Divide sts on 4 dpn and join to work in the rnd, being careful not to twist sts.
For rolled edge, knit 20 rnds.
Change to larger ndls.
Next rnd: *K12, pm, work cable over next 10 sts, p16, pm, work cable over next 10 sts, k12; rep from * once more.
Next 5 rnds: *K22, p16, k44, p16, k22.
Rep the last 6 rnds another 12 times, or until 2 balls of yarn are used up.

With hat inside out, arrange the sts on 2 needles so the purl sections are centered on the front and back of the hat. Join with 3-ndl BO. Turn the hat right side out.

Make 2 I-cords each 47¼ in / 120 cm long as follows: On short dpn, CO 4 sts. *Do not turn, slip sts to other end of dpn, draw yarn snugly across back of work and k4; rep from * until cord is desired length. Cut yarn and draw end through rem sts but do not tighten.

FINISHING

Beginning at the top of the hat, lace one cord through the cable twists as for lacing a shoe. Do not pull the cord too tight. When you reach the rolled edge, adjust the cord, shorten the ends if needed, and sew the ends to the inside of the hat. Repeat on second side.

Tip: You can also make I-cord using a knitting mill or spool.

Passion [DESIGNED BY MANUELA SEITTER]

LEVEL OF DIFFICULTY
 Easy

SIZE
Circumference 20½-22 in / 52-56 cm

MATERIALS
Yarn: (CYCA #6), Schachenmayr/SMC Kadina Light (62% acrylic, 26% wool, 12% polyester; 43 yd/39 m / 50 g), Ruby 32, 150 g

Needles: U.S. size 15 / 10 mm: set of 5 dpn

Large-eye darning needle

GAUGE
10 sts and 12 rows in ribbing = 4 x 4 in / 10 x 10 cm.

Adjust needle size to obtain correct gauge if necessary.

PATTERN STITCHES
Ribbing
All rnds: (K2, p2) around.

INSTRUCTIONS
CO 56 sts. Join to work in the rnd, being careful not to twist sts.

Work in ribbing until piece measures 13 in / 33 cm.

BO loosely in ribbing.

FINISHING
Thread darning needle with yarn.

On the 4th rnd from the CO edge, use the yarn to draw 2 columns of knit sts together by bringing the yarn from the inside of the hat on the right side of one rib, and back to the inside on the left side of the second rib. Join the 1st and 2nd ribs this way, the 3rd and 4th, 5th and 6th, and so forth around the hat. Fasten off.

On the 12th rnd from the CO edge, join ribbing above, but this time start by joining the 2nd and 3rd ribs, the 4th and 5th, and so on around the hat, ending by joining the last rib and the first rib. Fasten off.

Wrap the yarn around all of the sts 3 in / 8 cm from the top of the hat and tighten. Bury the yarn inside the hat.

Weave in ends.

Ring Around the Rosy [DESIGNED BY HEIKE ROLAND]

LEVEL OF DIFFICULTY
 Easy

SIZE
Circumference 21¼-22¾ in / 54-58 cm

MATERIALS
Yarn: (CYCA #4), Lana Grossa Merino Big Superfine (100% Merino; 131 yd/120 m / 50 g), Turquoise 910, Red 905, White 615, Petrol 911, Green 909, Orange 922 and Purple 695, 50 g each

Needles: U.S. size 7 / 4.5 mm: 24 in / 60 cm circular

GAUGE
20 sts and 28 rows in St st = 4 x 4 in / 10 x 10 cm.

Adjust needle size to obtain correct gauge if necessary.

PATTERN STITCHES
Stockinette Stitch (St st)
All rnds: Knit.

Ribbing
All rnds: (K1, p1) around.

INSTRUCTIONS
With Petrol, CO 120 sts. Join to work in the rnd, being careful not to twist sts. Place marker for beg of rnd.
Work 20 rnds in ribbing.

Change to St st and work in stripe sequence as follows:
*1 rnd White
6 rnds Red
1 rnd White
6 rnds Purple
1 rnd White
6 rnds Green
1 rnd White
6 rnds Orange
1 rnd White
6 rnds Turquoise
Rep from * for stripe pattern.

Work 37 rnds in stripe sequence, and then begin shaping cap as follows:
Rnd 38: (K18, k2tog) around—114 sts.
Every 4th rnd, dec 6 sts evenly around until 6 sts rem, with 1 less st between decreases on each dec rnd. For example,
Rnd 42: (K17, k2tog) around—108 sts.
Rnd 46: (K16, k2tog) around—102 sts.

FINISHING
Run the tail of yarn through rem sts twice and tighten to fasten off. Weave in ends.

Tassel: Wrap yarn approx. 20-50 times around a piece of cardboard that is approx. 3½ in / 9 cm wide (or around your palm). Wrap a piece yarn through all strands at the top of the tassel 3 or 4 times and knot tightly. Cut a piece of yarn about 12 in / 30 cm long and wrap it around all of the strands several times approx. ⅝ - ¾ in / 1.5-2 cm from the top of the tassel. Pull the ends through the loop into the tassel. Cut the tassel and trim evenly. Sew the tassel to the tip of the hat.

Braided tie: With all colors except Petrol, cut a length of yarn approx. 50 in / 130 cm long. Braid these strands together and knot the ends. Tie the braid around the hat in the seventh/purple stripe. Bury the ends inside the hat.

Understatement [DESIGNED BY JUTTA BÜCKER]

LEVEL OF DIFFICULTY

 Experienced

SIZE

Circumference 21¼ in / 54 cm

MATERIALS

Yarn: (CYCA #4), Zitron Gobi (40% Merino, 30% camel, 30% alpaca; 88 yd/80 m / 50 g), Charcoal 01, 100 g

Needles: U.S. size 8 / 5 mm: set of 5 dpn and 16 in / 40 cm circular

Cable needle

GAUGE

19 sts and 30 rows in Slip Stitch and rev St st = 4 x 4 in / 10 x 10 cm.

22 sts and 24 rows in Cable pattern = 4 x 4 in / 10 x 10 cm.

Adjust needle size to obtain correct gauge if necessary.

CHART

Page 92

PATTERN STITCHES

Cable Pattern

(Multiple of 8)

Work following chart. Only odd-numbered rnds are shown. On even-numbered rnds, knit the knits and purl the purls. Work the 8-st repeat around the hat. At beg of Rnd 11, slip the first 2 sts and work them as part of the 4-st cable at the end of the rnd.

Cuff Pattern

(Multiple of 5)

Row 1: Knit.

Row 2: Purl.

Row 3: *K5, holding working yarn to the side so it won't rotate with the sts, rotate sts on right ndl 360 degrees; rep from * around, ending with k5.

Slip Stitch Pattern

Rnd 1: (Sl 1 pw wyif, p1) around.

Rnd 2: Knit.

Rnd 3: (P1, sl 1 pw wyif) around.

Rnd 4: Knit.

Rep Rnds 1-4 for pattern.

Stockinette Stitch (St st)

All rnds: Knit.

Reverse Stockinette Stitch (rev St st)

All rnds: Purl.

Ribbing

All rnds: (K1, p1) around.

INSTRUCTIONS

With circular needle, CO 105 sts. Work 3 rows of Cuff pattern.

Join to work in the rnd being careful not to twist sts.

Work 12 rnds in Slip Stitch, then 4 rnds in rev St st.

Next rnd: (K7, M1) 15 times—120 sts.

Work 22 rnds in Cable Pattern following the chart: work Rnds 1-12 once, then Rnds 1-10 once more.

Work 5 rnds in rev St st, decreasing as follows on the first rnd: (K6, k2tog) 15 times—105 sts rem. On the 3rd rnd, (K15, k2tog) 6 times, k to end—99 sts rem.

On the 5th rnd, (K9, k2tog) 9 times, k to end—90 sts rem.

Work 6 rnds in Slip Stitch pattern, then 6 rnds in ribbing.

Next rnd: Change to dps and k2tog around to last st—45 sts rem.

FINISHING

Run the tail of yarn through rem sts twice and tighten to fasten off. Weave in ends.

Rose Petals [DESIGNED BY TANJA STEINBACH]

LEVEL OF DIFFICULTY

 Intermediate

SIZE

Circumference 21¼-22 in / 54-56 cm

MATERIALS

Yarn: (CYCA #4), Schachenmayr/SMC Aventica (65% acrylic, 25% wool, 10% polyamide; 131 yd/120 m / 50 g), Magenta Heather 97, 100 g

Needles: U.S. size 10 / 6 mm: 7 dpn

Cable needle

18 pearl beads, about 3 mm hole diameter

Sewing needle and thread or U.S. size B or C / 2 or 3 mm crochet hook (see Techniques)

GAUGE

16 sts and 24 rows in St st = 4 x 4 in / 10 x 10 cm.

Adjust needle size to obtain correct gauge if necessary.

TECHNIQUES

Attaching Beads with Crochet Hook

Slide 1 bead on the crochet hook, catch the stitch on which the bead is to be set with the crochet hook, and pull the stitch through the bead and the hook. Place the stitch back on the left needle and knit it normally. The bead sits at the base of the stitch.

PATTERN STITCHES

Stockinette Stitch (St st)
All rnds: Knit.

Cable Pattern
(Multiple of 4)

Work as charted. All rows are included in chart. The repeat is 8 sts. Work Rnds 1-23 once.

CHART

	23
	22
	21
	20
	19
	18
	17
	16
	15
	14
	13
	12
	11
	10
	9
	8
	7
	6
	5
	4
	3
	2
	1

rep = 4 to 8 sts

⊟ = purl

■ = knit

☐ = no stitch

Ⅴ = 3-in-1: (k1, yo, k1) into the same st

+ = M1: make 1 – lift strand between 2 sts and knit into back loop

∩ = S2KP: sl 2 sts tog kw, k1, p2sso

⊖ = knit with bead

= sl 1 to cn and hold in back, k1, p1 from cn

= sl 1 to cn and hold in front, p1, k1 from cn

= sl 2 to cn and hold in back, k1, k2 from cn

INSTRUCTIONS

CO 72 sts. Divide sts evenly on 4 dpn and join to work in the rnd, being careful not to twist sts. Work charted pattern. On Rnd 15, slip the first 2 sts of the rnd and work them as part of the cable at the end of the rnd. On Rnd 23, add the beads (see page 94).

Divide sts evenly over 6 dpn (24 sts per ndl) and work St st over all 144 sts.

When hat measures 5¼ in / 13 cm from CO edge, k2tog at the end of each ndl—138 sts rem.

Dec as above every rnd until 6 sts rem.

FINISHING

Run the tail of yarn through rem sts twice and tighten to fasten off. Weave in ends.

Dampen hat and stretch over a cardboard circle approx. 10¼-10¾ in / 26-27 cm in diameter; leave until completely dry.

Tip: The diameter of the circle should be approximately the same size as the St st portion of the hat.

Winter Dreams [DESIGNED BY WALTRAUD RÖHNER]

LEVEL OF DIFFICULTY

 Experienced

SIZE

Circumference 20½-21¼ in / 52-54 cm

MATERIALS

Yarn: (CYCA #1), Regia Twin (75% wool, 25% polyamide; 459 yd/420 m / 100 g), Janina Color 7318, 50 g

(CYCA #1), Regia Uni 4-ply (75% wool, 25% polyamide; 230 yd/210 m / 50 g), Light Gray Heather 1991, 50 g

Needles: U.S. size 1-2 / 2.5 mm: set of 5 dpn and circulars 16 in / 40 cm and 24 in / 60 cm

GAUGE

29 sts and 38 rows in St st = 4 x 4 in / 10 x 10 cm.

Adjust needle size to obtain correct gauge if necessary.

CHART

Page 93

PATTERN STITCHES

Stockinette Stitch (St st)
All rnds: Knit.

Star Pattern

Work as charted in St st. Work the 16-st rep 9 times around the hat, and work Rnds 1-24 once.

Dot Pattern

Work as charted in St st. The repeat is 4 sts and 4 rnds.

Grid Pattern

Work as charted in St st. The repeat is 2 sts, ending with 1 st at the end of the rnd. Work Rnds 1-4 once.

INSTRUCTIONS

With Janina Color and shorter circular ndl, CO 144 sts. Join to work in the rnd, being careful not to twist sts.

Facing: Knit 28 rnds.
Turning ridge: With Light Gray Heather, knit 1 rnd, purl 1 rnd, knit 1 rnd.

Brim: Work 24 rnds of Star pattern.

Sides: With Light Gray Heather, knit 1 rnd.
Next rnd: (K2, M1) around—216 sts.
Change to longer circular ndl and work 36 rnds in Dot Pattern.

Wheel: With Light Gray Heather, (K6, k2tog) around—189 sts rem.
Work rows 1-3 of Grid Pattern.
Next rnd: Work Rnd 4 of Grid pattern and (K2, k2tog) to last 9 sts, k9—144 sts rem.
Work 2 rnds in Light Gray Heather.
Next rnd: (K10, k2tog) around—132 sts rem.
Work 20 rnds in St st, dec as above every other rnd with 1 less st before each dec. *At the same time*, change colors as foll: *4 rnds Janina Color, 4 rnds in Light Gray Heather; rep from * once and end with 4 rnds Janina Color—12 sts rem.

Top Knot: Work even on these 12 sts for 5 in / 12 cm.
Next rnd: K2tog around—6 sts rem.

FINISHING

Run the tail of yarn through rem sts twice and tighten to fasten off. Weave in ends.
Fold the facing to the inside and stitch in place.
Tie the hat tip to make a knot.

Maverick [DESIGNED BY NADJA BRANDT]

LEVEL OF DIFFICULTY

 Intermediate

SIZE

Circumference 21¼-22¾ in / 54-58 cm

MATERIALS

Yarn: (CYCA #3), Austermann Murano Lace (53% wool, 47% acrylic; 437 yd/400 m / 100 g), Red 01, 100 g

Needles: U.S. size 4 / 3.5 mm: set of 5 dpn

GAUGE

22 sts and 29 rows in St st = 4 x 4 in / 10 x 10 cm.

Adjust needle size to obtain correct gauge if necessary.

PATTERN STITCHES

Ribbing

All rnds: (K2, p2) around.

Stockinette Stitch (St st)

All rnds: Knit.

Reverse Stockinette Stitch (rev St st)

All rnds: Purl.

Welt Pattern

Rnds 1-6: Work in St st.

Rnds 7-12: Work in rev St st.

Rep Rnds 1-12 for pattern.

INSTRUCTIONS

Loosely CO 120 sts. Divide sts evenly on 4 dpns and join to work in the rnd, being careful not to twist sts. Work 6 rnds in ribbing.

Set up patterns as follows:

Next rnd: Work 30 sts in ribbing, 30 sts in Welt pattern, 30 sts in ribbing, 30 sts Welt.

Work 43 rnds in patterns as set, ending after finishing 6 rnds of knit in Welt pattern.

Purl 1 rnd.

On the next rnd, work across the first 30 rib sts, then begin working back and forth on the following 30 Welt sts. Place the 2 sets of 30 rib sts on spare ndls.

Continuing in Welt Pattern as set, join the welt strip to rib sections on both sides as follows: At the end of each WS row, slip the next stitch from the adjacent ribbing section onto the working needle; turn. On the RS row, work the slipped stitch together with the first stitch of the Welt section. When joining a knit st, k2tog. When joining a purl st, p2tog. At the end of each RS row, work the last st of the Welt section together with the first of the held ribbing sts.

When 30 rows are completed, 15 sts have been decreased on each side.

Continue working back and forth on the 30 Welt sts and joining, but instead of slipping the first held st, at the end of every row, insert the needle into the st knitwise and pull the yarn through, but leave the stitch on the right needle. Work this new stitch together with the first st on RS rows and last st on WS rows instead of a slipped st. After another 30 rows with 15 decs on each side, the 30 sts of the front Welt panel and the 30 sts on the back Welt panel remain.

Carefully turn hat inside out and join the 2 sets of live sts with 3-ndl BO.

FINISHING

Weave in ends.

Study in Contrasts [DESIGNED BY ANJA BELLE]

LEVEL OF DIFFICULTY

 Experienced

SIZE

Circumference 21 in / 53 cm

MATERIALS

Yarn: (CYCA #1), Schachenmayr/SMC Baby Wool (100% Merino; 93 yd/85 m / 25 g), Black 99 and White 01, 50 g each

Needles: U.S. size 1-2 / 2.5 mm: 24 in / 60 cm circular

Cable needle

GAUGE

25 sts and 35 rows in Double Knitting = 4 x 4 in / 10 x 10 cm.

Adjust needle size to obtain correct gauge if necessary.

CHART

Maze Pattern

Work in Double Knitting following the chart. Work the 10-st rep, 12 times around the hat. Rep Rows 1-20 for pattern.

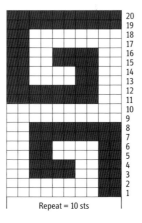

Repeat = 10 sts

▮ = Make 1 double st pair with Black as the foreground color
☐ = Make 1 double st pair with White as the foreground color

DOUBLE KNITTING

Cast on with both colors held together. Work following the chart. Each square stands for one double-stitch pair. A black square indicates a square worked as both yarns to back, k1 with Black; both yarns to front, p1 with White. A white square indicates a square worked as both yarns to back, k1 with White; both yarns to front, p1 with Black.

INSTRUCTIONS

With both colors held together, CO 120 sts. Join to work in the rnd, being careful not to twist sts. Begin working in Double Knitting and the Maze Pattern, working chart Rnds 1-20 three times, then Rnds 1-10 once more.

Now separate the sts so each color is on a separate ndl.

BO the inside and outside separately as follows: Divide the sts into 4 sections of 30 sts each, starting in the middle of the row of each color. Then split each section of 30 sts in half, with 15 sts on each ndl. Working from the outside toward the center, join the two halves with 3-ndl BO.

Turn the hat right side out, and make sure the edges are aligned neatly.

FINISHING

Weave in ends.

Quick Change Artist [DESIGNED BY SYLVIE RASCH]

LEVEL OF DIFFICULTY

 Intermediate

SIZE

Circumference 20½-23¾ in / 52-60 cm

MATERIALS

Yarn: (CYCA #1), Schoppel Zauberball (75% wool, 25% nylon; 459 yd/420 m / 100 g), Pause in Blue 2099, 150 g

Needles: U.S. size 4 (3.5 mm): 24 in / 60 cm circular

Cable needle

GAUGE

22 sts and 30 rows in St st = 4 x 4 in / 10 x 10 cm.

Adjust needle size to obtain correct gauge if necessary.

Tip: The hat can be opened up and worn as a cowl.

PATTERN STITCHES

Ribbing

All rnds: (K1, p1) around.

Eyelet Pattern

Row 1: K1, sl 1 wyif, k1, k2tog, yo, k5, knit the last st (11th st) tog with the first edge stitch of the knitted piece.

Rows 2 and 4: Sl 1, p8, k1, slip the last st pw.

Row 3: K1, sl 1 wyif, k8, knit the last st (11th st) tog with the first edge stitch of the knitted piece. Rep Rows 1-4 for pattern.

Tip: When increasing at the ribbing, it will be easier if you make the extra stitch with a cable needle or extra dpn.

INSTRUCTIONS

CO 100 sts. Join to work in the rnd, being careful not to twist sts; pm for beg of rnd.

Work in ribbing for 1 in / 2.5 cm.

Begin working back and forth using the dpn as follows:

Next row (RS): Work 3 sts in ribbing as set; turn.

Next row (WS): Sl 1, p2; turn.

*Next row (RS): K1, M1, knit to the slipped st, k2tog (slipped st and next stitch of ribbing); turn.

Next row (WS): Sl 1, purl.

Rep from * until the St st strip is 11 sts wide.

**Next row (RS): K10, k2tog (slipped st and next stitch of ribbing); turn.

Next row (WS): Sl 1, purl to end.

Rep from ** until all sts of ribbing have been joined to new St st strip.

***Next row (RS): K10, sl 1, in the next st on the edge of the previous strip pick up and knit 1, psso.

Next row (WS): Sl 1, purl to end.

Rep from *** until hat is desired length.

Note: There is one more 10-st wide section to work around, adding the eyelets.

Work Eyelet Pattern around until you are approx. 5 in / 12 cm from the first hole. Continue eyelet pattern and, *at the same time,* k2tog with every 4th and 5th st.

When the eyelet pattern has been worked all the way around and 4-5 sts rem, work I-cord as follows: *Knit to end; do not turn. Slide the stitches to the other end of the ndl, draw the yarn tightly across the back. Rep from * until the cord is about ¾ in / 2 cm long.

FINISHING

Run the tail of yarn through the eyelets and tighten. Make a pompom (see page 95) and sew to the end of the I-cord. Wash hat and dry to shape. Weave in ends.

Fairylike [DESIGNED BY HELGA SPITZ]

LEVEL OF DIFFICULTY

 Easy

SIZE

Circumference 22-22¾ in / 56-58 cm

MATERIALS

Yarn: (CYCA #4), Lana Grossa Alta Moda Alpaca (90% alpaca, 5% virgin wool, 5% polyamide; 153 yd/140 m / 50 g), Green 23, 50 g

(CYCA #4), Lana Grossa Babykid (60% mohair, 40% microfiber; 220 yd/210 m / 50 g), yellow-green 31, 50 g

Needles: U.S. size 10½ / 6 or 7 mm: set of 5 dpn

1 matching button (optional)

GAUGE

13 sts and 22 rows in St st with 1 strand Alpaca and 2 strands Babykid held tog = 4 x 4 in / 10 x 10 cm.

Adjust needle size to obtain correct gauge if necessary.

PATTERN STITCHES

Welt Pattern

Rnds 1-5: Rev St st.

Rnds 6-10: St st.

Rep Rnds 1-10 for pattern.

Reverse Stockinette Stitch (rev St st)

All rnds: Purl.

Stockinette Stitch (St st)

All rnds: Knit.

Note: Entire hat is worked with 1 strand of Alta Moda Alpaca and 2 strands of Babykid held together.

INSTRUCTIONS

With 1 strand of Alta Moda Alpaca and 2 strands of Babykid held tog, CO 56 sts. Divide sts evenly on 4 dpn and join to work in the rnd, being careful not to twist sts. Work 32 rnds in welt pattern.

Rnd 33: (K5, k2tog) around—48 sts rem.

Work 8 rnds in welt pattern.

Rnd 42: (K4, k2tog) around—40 sts rem.

Work 5 rnds in welt pattern.

Change to St st and dec every other rnd as foll:

Dec rnd 1: (K3, k2tog) around.

Dec rnd 2: (K2, k2tog) around.

Dec rnd 3: (K1, k2tog) around.

Dec rnd 4: (K2tog around)—8 sts rem.

FINISHING

Run the tail of yarn through rem sts twice and tighten to fasten off. Weave in ends.

Sew a matching button to the side of the hat for extra decoration.

Daredevil [DESIGNED BY MONIKA ECKERT]

LEVEL OF DIFFICULTY

 Experienced

SIZE

Circumference 22-22¾ in / 56-58 cm

MATERIALS

Yarn: (CYCA #3), Zitron Life Style (100% Merino; 169 yd/155 m / 50 g), Petrol 81, 100 g

Needles: U.S. size 4 / 3.5 mm: set of 5 dpn and two 24 in / 60 cm circulars

Cable needle

GAUGE

14 sts and 40 rows in Triangle pattern = 2½ in x 4 in / 6.5 cm x 10 cm.

Adjust needle size to obtain correct gauge if necessary.

PATTERN STITCHES

Triangle Pattern

Work following chart. Only odd-numbered rnds are shown. On even-numbered rnds, knit the knits and purl the purls and yarnovers. The repeat is 8 sts. Work rows 1-76 once.

INSTRUCTIONS

With dpn, CO 8 sts. Divide evenly on 4 ndls and join to knit in the rnd, being careful not to twist sts. Knit 1 rnd.

Work Triangle pattern chart 8 times around.

Continue, following chart. When sts no longer fit on dpn, switch to circular needles.

After Rnd 75, BO loosely.

FINISHING

Weave in ends.

Repeat = 14 sts after Rnd 25

■ = knit
○ = yo
◢ = k2tog
« = ssk
– = purl
▲ = sl 1 kw, k2tog, psso
⋁ = kf&b

Far North [DESIGNED BY LYDIA KLÖS]

LEVEL OF DIFFICULTY

Experienced

SIZE
Circumference 22-22¾ in / 56-58 cm

MATERIALS
Yarn: Weight (CYCA #3), Schachenmayr/SMC Universa (55% Merino, 45% acrylic; 136 yd/124 m / 50 g), Natural White 102, Cherry 32, and Navy Blue 150, 50 g each

Needles: U.S. size 2-3 / 3 mm: 9 dpn or 2 circular needles

Stitch markers (for using with circular ndls)

GAUGE
25 sts and 33 rows in St st = 4 x 4 in / 10 x 10 cm.

Adjust needle size to obtain correct gauge if necessary.

CHART
Page 92

PATTERN STITCHES

Ribbing
All rnds: (K1, p1) around.

Stockinette Stitch (St st)
All rnds: Knit.

Norwegian Pattern
Work in St st following chart. Carry the unused color loosely across the back of the work and weave it in for long carries. Work the 14-st repeat 8 times around. Work Rnds 1-67 once.

INSTRUCTIONS
With Cherry CO 112 sts. Divide sts on 8 dpn or 2 circs and join to knit in the rnd, being careful not to twist sts.
Work 6 rnds of ribbing. Work Norwegian pattern in St st, following chart.

FINISHING
Run the tail of yarn through rem 8 sts twice and tighten to fasten off. Weave in ends.

Tip: If working on 2 circular ndls, use stitch markers to separate chart repeats.

A Day in Paris [DESIGNED BY UTE DORNHOF]

LEVEL OF DIFFICULTY

 Easy

SIZE

Circumference 21¼-22 in / 54-56 cm

MATERIALS

Yarn: (CYCA #3), Schachenmayr/SMC Extra Merino (100% Merino; 142 yd/130 m / 50 g), Charcoal Heather 97, 250 g; Natural White 2, Violet 48, and Lavender 47, small amounts

Needles: U.S. size 10 / 6 mm

Crochet hook: U.S. size G-6 / 4 mm

Brooch pin jewelry finding

GAUGE

14 sts and 20 rows in St st with yarn doubled = 4 x 4 in / 10 x 10 cm.

Adjust needle size to obtain correct gauge if necessary.

PATTERN STITCHES

Ribbing

All rows: (K1, p1) across.

Seed Stitch

Row 1 (RS): (K2, p2) around.

Row 2: (P2, k2) around.

Rep Rnds 1 and 2 for pattern.

Note: Yarn is used doubled throughout.

INSTRUCTIONS

With two strands of Charcoal Heather held tog, CO 64 sts. Work back and forth in ribbing for 2½ in / 6 cm.

Knit 1 row, inc 28 sts evenly across.

Begin working in Seed st. When hat measures 5½ in / 14 cm from CO edge, begin shaping.

In the next row and then every other row 3 more times, dec 10 sts evenly across. Next, on every other row twice, dec 13 sts evenly across; finally, in the next row, k2tog across.

Run the tail of yarn through rem sts tighten to fasten off.

FINISHING

Sew back seam. Weave in ends.

Crochet Flower Brooch

Outer petals:

With White, Ch 5 and join into a ring with 1 sl st to first ch.

Rnd 1: (Ch 2, 1 dc around ring) 9 times, sl st to join.

Rnd 2: In each ch loop, work (1 sc, ch 1, 1 dc, ch 1, 1 sc), sl st to join—10 petals created. Fasten off. Turn.

Rnd 3 (worked on WS): Join Violet and work 1 sc in 1st dc, (ch 3, 1 sc in next dc) round—10 ch loops.

Rnd 4: In each ch loop around, work (1 sc, ch 1, 2 dc, ch 1, 1 sc); sl st to join—10 petals.

Inner petals:

With Lavender, Ch 5. Sl st to first ch to form a ring.

Rnd 1: Ch 2, work 9 dc around ring, sl st to join.

Rnd 2, Picot edging: *1 sc, ch 3, and then work 1 sc in the first ch; rep from * 9 times.

Center:

With Charcoal, ch 5. Sl st to first ch to form a ring.

Rnd 1: Work 6 sc around ring. Sl st to join.

Rnd 2: With White, work 1 sc in each sc. Sl st to join.

Sew the inner petals and center onto the outer petals, using the photo as a guide. Weave in ends.

Tip: Try making the flower in several different colors so you can change the hat to match your outfit!

Surf's Up [DESIGNED BY FRAUKE KIEDAISCH]

LEVEL OF DIFFICULTY

 Easy

SIZE

Circumference 21¼-22¾ in / 54-58 cm

MATERIALS

Yarn: (CYCA #6), SMC Select Highland Alpaca (50% alpaca, 50% wool; 44 yd/40 m / 50 g), Jade 2968 and Pigeon 2962, 100 g each

Needles: U.S. size 15 / 10 mm: set of 5 dpn and 24 in / 60 cm circular

Stitch markers

GAUGE

8 sts and 10 rnds in Wave pattern = 4 x 4 in / 10 x 10 cm.

Adjust needle size to obtain correct gauge if necessary.

PATTERN STITCHES

Ribbing

All rnds: (K1, p1) around.

Wave Pattern

(Multiple of 10)

Rnd 1: With Jade, purl.
Rnd 2: With Jade, *k5, (k1, yo) twice, k1, yo twice, (k1 yo) twice; rep from * around.
Rnd 3: With Pigeon, purl, dropping the yarnovers.
Rnd 4: With Pigeon, *(k1, yo) twice, k1, yo twice, (k1, yo) twice, k5; rep from * around.
Rnd 5: With Jade, purl, dropping the yarnovers.
Rep Rnds 2-5 for pattern.

Stockinette Stitch (St st)

All rnds: Knit around.

INSTRUCTIONS

With dpn and Pigeon, CO 36 sts. Divide sts evenly on 4 dpns (9 sts per ndl) and join to work in the rnd, being careful not to twist sts.
Work 3 rnds in ribbing.
Change to circular ndl, pm for beg of rnd.
Next rnd: (K9, M1) around—40 sts.
Work 17 rnds of Wave pattern (the 17th rnd is Rnd 5 of pattern).

CROWN SHAPING

With Jade, work in St st and dec as follows, changing to dpn when sts no longer fit on circ:
Rnd 1: (K2, k2tog) around—30 sts.
Rnd 2: Knit.
Rnd 3: (K1, k2tog) around—20 sts (5 per ndl).
Rnd 4: Knit.
Rnd 5: K2tog around—10 sts rem.

FINISHING

Run the tail of yarn through rem sts and tighten to fasten off. Weave in ends.
Make a 4-6 in / 10-15 cm pompom (see page 95) and sew to top of hat.

Tip: To make the hat fit more snugly, knit the first rnd with transparent elastic thread.

Red Sunrise [DESIGNED BY DAGMAR BERGK]

PATTERN STITCHES

Basketweave Stitch

Worked back and forth as charted. Row 1 is a WS row. Rep Rows 1-8 for pattern.

Stockinette Stitch (St st)

All rnds: Knit.

INSTRUCTIONS

The band is worked sideways in Basketweave pattern. When casting on, make a tail long enough to use to sew the ends together for the back seam.

BRIM

With crochet hook, ch 30 for provisional CO (see page 94).

With the circular needle, pick up and knit 37sts through the back of the crochet chain.

Work Rows 1-8 of Basketweave chart 14 times, then work Rows 1-7 one more time. Do not BO. Remove the provisional CO and join brim with Kitchener stitch (see page 95).

BODY

With RS facing, pick up and knit 88 sts along the edge of the brim that does not have the garter edge sts as follows: *pick up and knit 1 st in each of the next 3 rows, skip 1 row; rep from * around. Join to work in the round.

Work 16 rnds of St st.

CROWN SHAPING

Rnd 1: (K9, k2tog) around.

Rnds 2, 4 and 6: Knit.

Rnd 3: (K8, k2tog) around.

Rnd 5: (K7, k2tog) around.

Rnd 7: (K6, k2tog) around.

Rnd 8: (K5, k2tog) around.

Rnd 9: (K4, k2tog) around.

Rnd 10: (K3, k2tog) around.

Rnd 11: (K2, k2tog) around.

Rnd 12: (K1, k2tog) around.

Rnd 13: K2tog around—8 sts rem.

FINISHING

Run the tail of yarn through rem sts and tighten to fasten off. Weave in ends.

Pattern Repeat = 27 sts

■ = knit on RS, purl on WS

● = knit every row for edge

= sl 3 to cn and hold in back, k3, k3 from cn

= sl 3 to cn and hold in front, k3, k3 from cn

Fresh Breeze [DESIGNED BY RENATE HOLZMANN]

LEVEL OF DIFFICULTY

 Intermediate

SIZE

Circumference 21-21¾ in / 53-55 cm

MATERIALS

Yarn: (CYCA #2), Lana Grossa Cool Wool 2000 (100% Merino; 175 yd/160 m / 50 g), in Turquoise 502 and Light Green 509, 50 g each

Needles: U.S. size 4 / 3.5 mm: set of 5 dpn

GAUGE

26 sts and 33 rows in St st = 4 x 4 in / 10 x 10 cm.

Adjust needle size to obtain correct gauge if necessary.

PATTERN STITCHES

Ribbing

All rnds: (K1, p1) around.

Stockinette Stitch (St st)

All rnds: Knit.

INSTRUCTIONS

With Turquoise, CO 120 sts. Divide sts evenly onto 4 dpn and join to work in the rnd, being careful not to twist sts.

Rnds 1-13: Work in ribbing.

Rnds 14-15: Knit.

Rnds 16-19: (With Green k4, with Turquoise k4) around.

Rnds 20-23: With Green k3, (with Turquoise k4, with Green k4) around, ending with Green k1.

Rnds 24-27: With Green k2, (with Turquoise k4, with Green k4) around, ending with Green k2.

Rnds 28-31: With Green k1, (with Turquoise k4, with Green k4) around, ending with Green k3.

Rnds 32-35: (With Turquoise k4, with Green k4) around.

Rnds 36-39: With Turquoise k3, (with Green k4, with Turquoise k4) around, ending with Turquoise k1.

Rnds 40-43: With Turquoise k2, (with Green k4, with Turquoise k4) around, ending with Turquoise k2.

Rnds 44-47: With Turquoise k1, (with Green k4, with Turquoise k4) around, ending with Turquoise k3.

Rnds 48-51: (With Green k4, with Turquoise k4) around.

CROWN SHAPING

Rnd 52: Rnd 52: With Green k3, (with Turquoise k4, with Green k4) around, ending with Green k1.

Rnd 53: With Green k1, k2tog (with Turquoise k2, k2tog, with Green k2, k2tog) around, ending with Green k1 – 90 sts rem.

Rnds 54-55: With Green k2, (with Turquoise k3, with Green k3) around, ending with Green k1.

Rnd 56: With Green, k1, (with Turquoise, k3, with Green, k2tog, k1) around, ending with Green, k2tog—75 sts rem.

Rnd 57: With Green k1, (with Turquoise k1, k2tog, with Green k2) around, ending with Green k1—60 sts rem.

Rnd 58-59: With Green k1, (with Turquoise k2, with Green k2) around, ending with Green k1.

Rnds 60: (With Turquoise k2, with Green k2) around.

Rnd 61: (With Turquoise k2tog, with Green k2tog) around—30 sts rem.

Rnd 62: With Turquoise, k2tog around—15 sts rem.

FINISHING

Run the tail of yarn through rem sts and tighten to fasten off. Weave in ends.

Either, Or [DESIGNED BY SARAH BASAS]

LEVEL OF DIFFICULTY

 Experienced

SIZE

Circumference 21¾-23¾ in / 55-60 cm

MATERIALS

Yarn: (CYCA #4), Lana Grossa Cool Wool Big (100% Merino; 131 yd/120 m / 50 g), Light Gray Heather 928, 100 g; small amounts of White 615 and Black 627

Needles: U.S. size 7 / 4.5 mm: set of 5 dpn

Cable needle

GAUGE

25 sts and 32 rows in St st = 4 x 4 in / 10 x 10 cm.

Adjust needle size to obtain correct gauge if necessary.

CHARTS

Page 93

PATTERN STITCHES

Small Cable

Work as charted for all rnds. Repeat chart Rows 1-3 for pattern.

Large Cable

Work as charted for all rnds. Repeat chart Rows 1-16 for pattern.

Half Brioche

Rnd 1: *K1, (yo, p1); rep from * to end of rnd.
Rnd 2: *K1, (purl yo and st tog); rep from * to end of rnd.

Stockinette Stitch (St st)

All rnds: Knit.

Reverse Stockinette Stitch (rev St st)

All rnds: Purl.

Argyle

Work in St st in colors as charted. Rep Rnds 1-25 for pattern.

INSTRUCTIONS

With Light Gray Heather, CO 96 sts. Divide sts evenly onto 4 dpn (24 sts per ndl) and join to work in the rnd, being careful not to twist sts.

BRIM

Work in Half Brioche for 60 rnds.

PATTERNS

Next rnd: Work 25 sts in Argyle, 11 sts in Small Cable, 3 sts in rev St st, 1 st in St st, 4 sts in rev St st, 33 sts in Large Cable, 4 sts in rev St st, 1 st in St st, 3 sts in rev St st, 11 sts in Small Cable. Work in pattern as set for 92 rnds.

CROWN SHAPING

Dec rnd: On ndl 1, *ssk, work to last 2 sts, k2tog; rep from * on each ndl—8 sts decreased. Rep dec rnd on every rnd until 16 sts rem, continuing in pattern between decreases.

FINISHING

Run the tail of yarn through rem sts and tighten to fasten off. Weave in ends.

Charleston [DESIGNED BY UTE DORNHOF]

LEVEL OF DIFFICULTY
 Intermediate

SIZE
Circumference 22½ in / 57 cm

MATERIALS
Yarn: (CYCA #4), Schachenmayr/SMC Aventica (65% acrylic, 25% wool, 10% nylon; 131 yd/120 m / 50 g), Passion 81, 100 g

Needles: U.S. size 10 / 6 mm: straight needles and set of 5 dpn

Crochet hook: U.S. size H-8 / 5 mm

Cable needle

GAUGE
15 sts and 28 rows in St st = 4 x 4 in / 10 x 10 cm.

Adjust needle size to obtain correct gauge if necessary

PATTERN STITCHES
Stockinette Stitch (St st)
All rnds: Knit.

Cable Pattern
Rows 1, 3, and 5: K1 (selvage), (p2, k4) to last 2 sts, p1, k1 (selvage).
Rows 2 and 4: Knit the knits and purl the purls.
Row 6: K1, *p2, sl 2 to cn and hold in front, k2, k2 from cn; rep from * to last 2 sts, p1, k1.
Rep Rows 1-6 for pattern.

INSTRUCTIONS
With straight ndls, CO 33.

BAND
Work Rows 1-6 of Cable Pattern 19 times, then work Rows 1-4 once more. BO.
Sew the CO and BO edges of the band together to form a ring.

CROWN
With dpn, CO 100 sts. Divide evenly on 4 dpn (25 sts per ndl) and join to work in the rnd, being careful not to twist sts.
Work 3 rnds in St st.
K2tog at beg and end of each ndl every 3rd rnd 4 times, then every other rnd 6 times, then every rnd twice.

FINISHING
Run the tail of yarn through rem sts and tighten to fasten off. Weave in ends.
Sew the Crown to the selvage edge of the Band with the seam on the left side.

CROCHET FLOWER
With crochet hook, ch 5 and end with sl st to 1st ch to join into a ring.
Rnd 1: Ch 4 (= 1 dc + 2 ch), (1 dc around ring, ch 2) 8 times; join with sl st to 2nd ch at beg (= total of 9 dc around).
Rnd 2: Work (1 sc, ch 1, 1 dc, ch 1, 1 sc) into each loop. Sl st to 1st sc to join.
Turn work.
Rnd 3: In the 1st dc, work *1 sc, ch 3. Repeat * from * in each dc around = 10 loops.
Rnd 4: In each loop work 1 sc, ch 1, 2 dc, ch 1, 1 sc. Sl st to join.
Now work the flower center. Bring the yarn through the middle to the front.
Rnd 1: In each dc around, work 1 sc, ch 1. Sl st to join.
Rnd 2: In each ch loop around, work (1 sc, ch 3, 1 sc).
Cut yarn and sew flower to left side of hat.

Pretty & Casual [DESIGNED BY URSULA AND MELANIE MARXER]

LEVEL OF DIFFICULTY

 Intermediate

SIZE

Circumference 20½-21¾ in / 52-55 cm

MATERIALS

Yarn: (CYCA #6), Lana Grossa Ragazza Lei (100% Merino; 43 yd/39 m / 50 g), Yellow 020, 150 g

Needles: U.S. size 15 / 10 mm: set of 5 dpn

Cable needle

GAUGE

10 sts and 16 rows in Half Brioche Stitch = 4 x 4 in / 10 x 10 cm.

Adjust needle size to obtain correct gauge if necessary.

PATTERN STITCHES

Ribbing

All rnds: (K1, p1) around.

Half Brioche Stitch

Rnd 1: (K1, p1) around.

Rnd 2: (K1 in st below, p1) around.

Rep Rnds 1 and 2 for pattern.

Reverse Stockinette Stitch (rev St st)

All rnds: Purl.

Cable Pattern

Work following chart. Only odd-numbered rnds are shown. On even rnds, knit the knits and purl the purls. Begin with the first st, work the 6-st rep 4 times around, then end with the last st. Rep Rows 1-8 for pattern.

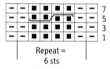

Repeat = 6 sts

 = purl

■ = knit

■■/■■ = sl 2 sts to cable needle and hold in back, k2 and then k2 from cn.

INSTRUCTIONS

CO 56 sts. Divide evenly on 4 dpn and join to work in the rnd, being careful not to twist sts. Work ribbing for 5 rnds.

Next rnd: Work 31 sts in Half Brioche Stitch, M1, work 26 sts in Cable Pattern.

Work 30 rnds in patterns as set.

CROWN SHAPING

Rnd 31: In the center of the Half Brioche section, k2tog before and after the center knit stitch, working the rest of the section in pattern as set. Work 2 rnds even.

Rnd 34: *Work 5 sts in Half Brioche as set, k3tog, work 6 sts in Half Brioche; rep from * once more, work last st of Half Brioche. In the cable section, p2tog in the spaces between each cable. Work 1 rnd even.

Rnd 36: In the center of the 25 rem Half Brioche sts, k2tog before and after the center stitch.

Remaining Rnds: K2tog around continuously until 8 sts rem.

FINISHING

Run the tail of yarn through rem sts and tighten to fasten off. Weave in ends.

Mysterious [DESIGNED BY DAGMAR BERGK]

LEVEL OF DIFFICULTY

 Experienced

SIZE

Circumference 20½-21¼ in / 52-54 cm

MATERIALS

Yarn: (CYCA #5), Rowan Cocoon (80% Merino, 20% mohair; 126 yd/115 m / 100 g), Seascape 813 or Quarry Tile 81, 100 g

Needles: U.S. size 10 / 6 mm: circular needle

Cable needle

Crochet hook: U.S. size J-10 / 6 mm for provisional CO

GAUGE

14 sts and 20 rows in Moss stitch = 4 x 4 in / 10 x 10 cm.

Adjust needle size to obtain correct gauge if necessary.

CHART

Page 92

PATTERN STITCHES

Cable Pattern

Work cable pattern as charted. Only RS rows are shown. On WS rows, knit the knits and purl the purls. Work Rows 1-56 twice, then work Row 1 once more.

Moss Stitch

Rnds 1 and 2: (K1, p1) around.
Rnds 3 and 4: (P1, k1) around.
Rep Rnds 1-4 for pattern.

INSTRUCTIONS

With crochet hook, ch 20 for provisional CO (see page 94).

With the circular needle, pick up and knit 14 sts through the back of the crochet chain, leaving a tail long enough to use to sew the ends of the band tog later.

Work in cable pattern. Do not BO. Remove the provisional CO and join the ends of the band with Kitchener stitch (see page 95).

With RS facing, pick up and knit 84 sts as foll:
*Pick up and knit 1 st in each of the next 3 rows, skip 1 row; rep from * around.

Work 20 rnds in Moss stitch.

CROWN SHAPING

Next rnd: (Work 12 sts in Moss st, k2tog) around, maintaining Moss st between decreases.

Continue to dec in this fashion, working 1 st less before each dec on every rnd until 6 sts rem.

FINISHING

Run the tail of yarn through rem sts and tighten to fasten off. Weave in ends.

Mitered Squares Around [DESIGNED BY EWA JOSTES]

LEVEL OF DIFFICULTY
 Intermediate

SIZE
Circumference 23¾ in / 60 cm

MATERIALS
Yarn: (CYCA #5), Schoppel-Wolle Pur (100% wool; 164 yd/150 m / 100 g), Halloween 2145, 100 g

Needles: U.S. size 8 / 5 mm: set of 5 dpn

Stitch markers

GAUGE
1 square of 25 sts = 3¼ in / 8 cm.

Adjust needle size to obtain correct gauge if necessary.

PATTERN STITCHES
Garter Stitch

Rnd 1: Knit.

Rnd 2: Purl.

Rep Rnds 1-2 for pattern.

Square

The squares are worked back and forth.

Row 1: K11, k3tog, k11.

Row 2 (and all even-numbered rows): Knit.

Row 3: K10, k3tog, k10.

Continue to dec in the center of each RS row, working 1 st less before and after the center k3tog decrease each time. Fasten off when 1 st remains.

INSTRUCTIONS
The hat is worked with a strip of 6 squares, and then is continued in the round. Do not cut the yarn. Begin with a tail of yarn long enough to sew a 72-stitch seam later.

SQUARE
Square 1: CO 25 sts and knit 1 square.

Square 2: Holding the finished square in your left hand, with the diagonal decrease line running from bottom right to top left, and the working needle in your right hand, pick up and knit 11 sts along the left edge of the square—12 sts. Using the backward loop cast-on, CO 13—25 sts total. Knit square.

Create 4 more squares as for Square 2—6 squares total.

CROWN
Pick up and knit 11 sts from each square—66 sts total. Divide sts evenly on 3 dpn (22 sts per ndl), placing a marker after the 11th st in the center of each needle.

*Work 4 rnds in Garter st.

Next rnd: Knit around, working k2tog before each marker and at the end of each ndl—6 sts decreased.

Purl 1 rnd.

Rep from * 2 more times.

Dec as above every rnd until 6 sts rem. Put all sts on 1 dpn.

Work I-cord on rem 6 sts as follows: *K6, do not turn; slide sts to other end of dpn; bring yarn across back and rep from * until 20 rows have been completed.

Fasten off.

FINISHING
Sew the seam on the square stripe.

On the bottom edge of the band of squares, pick up and knit 13 sts in each square—78 sts total.

Work 8 rnds in Garter st. BO loosely.

Tie a knot in the I-cord. Weave in ends.

On Fire [DESIGNED BY URSULA AND MELANIE MARXER]

LEVEL OF DIFFICULTY

 Intermediate

SIZE

Circumference 20½-21¾ in / 52-55 cm

MATERIALS

Yarn: (CYCA #6), Lana Grossa Ragazza Lei
(100% Merino; 43 yd/39 m / 50 g), Orange
23, 250 g

Needles: U.S. size 17 / 12 mm: straight
needles and U.S. size 15 / 10 mm: set of 5 dpn

GAUGE

11 sts and 13 rows in Ribbing on smaller
needles = 4 x 4 in / 10 x 10 cm.

Adjust needle sizes to obtain correct gauge if
necessary.

CHART

Cable Pattern

Work as charted. Only RS rows are shown. On WS
rows, knit the knits and purl the purls. Rep Rows
1-12 for pattern.

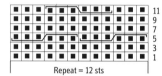

Repeat = 12 sts

■ = knit

■■■■/■■■ = Sl 3 to cn and hold at back, k3,
k3 from cn

■■■■■■■ = Sl 3 to cn and hold at front, k3,
k3 from cn

PATTERN STITCHES

Ribbing

All rows: (P2, k1) around.

Garter Stitch

All rows: Knit.

INSTRUCTIONS

Tip: The Cable panel is worked with a double
strand of yarn.

BAND

With 2 strands of yarn held tog and larger
needles, CO 18 sts.

Setup row: K1 (selvage), work 3 sts in Garter st,
work 12 sts in Cable Pattern, p1, k1 (selvage).
Work in pattern as set for 60 rows. BO. Sew CO
and BO ends of band tog with Kitchener stitch to
form a ring (see page 95).

CROWN

With RS facing and edge of cable with the purl st
on top, use dpn to pick up and knit 54 sts around
band. Join to work in the round.
Work 8 rnds in p2, k1 ribbing.

Next rnd: (P2tog, k1) around.
Work 4 rnds p1, k1 ribbing.

Next rnd: Knit each purl st tog with the following
knit st.

Next 2 rnds: K2tog around.

FINISHING

Run the tail of yarn through rem sts and tighten
to fasten off. Weave in ends.

Make a pompom (see page 95) and sew it to the
top of the hat.

Child's Play [DESIGNED BY STEFANIE THOMAS]

LEVEL OF DIFFICULTY

 Experienced

SIZE

Circumference 21¼-22 in / 54-56 cm

MATERIALS

Yarn: (CYCA #4), Lana Grossa Cool Wool Big (100% Merino; 131 yd/120 m / 50 g), Turquoise 910, Peony 690, White 615, Charcoal 618, Green 909, and Orange 922, 50 g each

Needles: U.S. size 7 / 4.5 mm: set of 5 dpn or 24 in / 60 cm circular

GAUGE

24 sts and 26 rows in St st over charted color pattern = 4 x 4 in / 10 x 10 cm.

Adjust needle size to obtain correct gauge if necessary.

CHART

Color Pattern

Work in St st following the chart. The repeat is 8 sts; work Rnds 1-25 once.

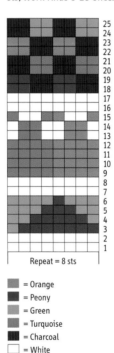

Repeat = 8 sts

▨ = Orange
■ = Peony
▨ = Green
▨ = Turquoise
■ = Charcoal
□ = White

PATTERN STITCHES

Stockinette Stitch (St st)
All rnds: Knit.

Ribbing
All rnds: (K1, p1) around.

INSTRUCTIONS

With Charcoal, CO 112 sts. Join to work in the rnd, being careful not to twist sts.

Work the following stripe sequence in ribbing: 5 rnds Charcoal, 2 rnds Orange, 2 rnds Charcoal, 2 rnds Turquoise, and 5 rnds Charcoal.

Work charted pattern in St st, working the 8-st repeat 14 times around.

After the last row of the chart, knit 2 rnds in White.

Continue in St st.

Next rnd: With Turquoise, (k5, k2tog) around—96 sts.

With White, knit 1 rnd.

Next rnd: With Orange, (k4, k2tog) around—80 sts.

With White, knit 1 rnd.

Next rnd: With Green, (k3, k2tog) around—64 sts.

Knit 1 rnd White, 1 rnd Peony, 2 rnds White.

Next rnd: With Turquoise, (k6, k2tog) around—56 sts.

Knit 1 rnd Turquoise.

Next rnd: With Orange, (k5, k2tog) around—48 sts.

Knit 1 rnd with Orange.

Next rnd: With Green, (k4, k2tog) around—40 sts.

Knit 1 rnd with Green.

Knit 2 rnds Peony, 2 rnds White.

FINISHING

Run the tail of yarn through rem sts and tighten to fasten off. Weave in ends.

With White, make a 2½ in / 6 cm pompom (see page 95) and sew it to the top of the hat.

Frost Flower [DESIGNED BY FRIEDERIKE PFUND]

LEVEL OF DIFFICULTY
 Intermediate

SIZE
Circumference 21¼ in / 54 cm

MATERIALS
Yarn: (CYCA #1), Regia Design Line Hand-dye Effect (70% wool, 25% nylon, 5% acrylic; 459 yd/420 m / 100 g), Rock Garden 885), 200 g

(CYCA #1), Regia Design Line (75% wool, 25% nylon; 230 yd/210 m / 50 g), Delphinium 2904, 200 g

Needles: U.S. sizes 6 / 4 mm and 7 / 4.5 mm: 24 in / 60 cm circulars

GAUGE
20 sts and 27 rows in St st with larger needles and doubled yarn, = 4 x 4 in / 10 x 10 cm.

Adjust needle sizes to obtain correct gauge if necessary.

PATTERN STITCHES
Stockinette Stitch (St st)
Row 1 (RS): Knit.
Row 2: Purl.
Rep Rows 1-2 for pattern.

Note: This hat is worked with two strands of yarn (one of each color) held together.

INSTRUCTIONS

With larger circular and 1 strand of each color held tog, CO 42 sts.
Work back and forth in St st for approx. 16 in / 40 cm.
Continue in St st and inc 1 st at each side (inside an edge st) on every 8th row 28 times—98 sts.
Pull out a 50 in / 125 cm length of yarn and run it through all sts on the ndl as a marker.
Work even in St st for another 8 in / 20 cm.
Change to smaller circular and work even in St st for another 8 in / 20 cm.
Do not BO.

Sew the long edges of the hat tog.
Fold the bottom edge 8 in / 20 cm to the inside so the live sts align with the yarn placed as a marker. Sew each live stitch to the corresponding stitch in the marked row. Do not make the seam too tight. The hat should remain elastic.

FINISHING
Make a pompom approx. 3 in / 8-9 cm in diameter (see page 95) and sew to tip of hat. Weave in ends.

Wear the hat with the seam in the back. Fold up the brim and wrap the rest of the hat around your neck as a scarf.

In a Playful Mood [DESIGNED BY MANUELA SEITTER]

LEVEL OF DIFFICULTY

 Easy

SIZE

Circumference 20½-22 in / 52-56 cm

MATERIALS

Yarn: Weight (CYCA #6), Schachenmayr/SMC Bravo Big (100% acrylic; 131 yd/120 m / 200 g), Natural 102, Neon Yellow 8232, Neon Orange 827) Neon Pink 8234, 200 g each

Needles: U.S. size 17 / 12 mm: set of 5 dpn

GAUGE

10 sts and 12 rows in St st = 4 x 4 in / 10 x 10 cm.

Adjust needle size to obtain correct gauge if necessary.

PATTERN STITCHES

Ribbing

All rnds: (K1, p1) around.

Stockinette Stitch (St st)

All rnds: Knit.

INSTRUCTIONS

With Natural, CO 32 sts. Divide sts evenly on dpn and join to work in the rnd, being careful not to twist sts.

Work 6 rnds in Ribbing.

Work stripes as follows:

Rnd 1: With Natural, knit.

Rnd 2: With Neon Yellow, purl.

Rnds 3-7: With Neon Yellow, knit.

Rnd 8: With Natural, purl.

Rnd 9: With Natural, knit.

Rnd 10: With Neon Pink, purl.

Rnds 11-14: With Neon Pink, knit.

Rnd 15: With Neon Orange, purl.

Rnd 16: With Neon Orange, knit.

Rnds 17-19: With Neon Orange knit and, in each rnd, dec 8 sts evenly around—8 sts rem.

FINISHING

Run the tail of yarn through rem sts and tighten to fasten off. Weave in ends.

Make a 4 in / 10 cm diameter pompom (see page 95) and sew it to the top of the hat.

Tip: You can make several hats with 200 g of each color. You will use approx. 50 g of each color per hat.

Chaotic [DESIGNED BY NADJA BRANDT]

LEVEL OF DIFFICULTY
Intermediate

SIZE
Circumference 19¾-21¼ in / 50-54 cm

MATERIALS
Yarn: (CYCA #1), Zitron Trekking XXL (75% wool, 25% polyamide; 459 yd/420 m / 100 g), Light Green 483, 100 g

Needles: U.S. size 4 / 3.5 mm: set of 5 dpn

Stitch markers

GAUGE
26 sts and 40 rows in St st = 4 x 4 in / 10 x 10 cm.

Adjust needle size to obtain correct gauge if necessary.

PATTERN STITCHES
Ribbing
All rnds: (K2, p2) around.

Stockinette Stitch (St st)
All rnds: Knit.

INSTRUCTIONS
CO 116 sts and divide sts evenly onto 4 dpn. Join to work in the rnd, being careful not to twist sts. Work 8 rnds in ribbing, then 8 rnds in St st.

TUCKS
First tuck: *K82, then count 8 rnds down and lift the st directly below the next st up onto the left ndl. Knit this tog with the following st. Rep from * 9 times. Knit to the end of the rnd.
Work 8 rnds even (count from the tuck, which is easily seen on the WS).
Work 3 more tucks in this fashion, with fewer rnds in each tuck as foll:
- **2nd tuck:** count 6 rounds down and work 7 rnds plain after the tuck rnd
- **3rd tuck:** count 5 rounds down and work 6 rnds plain after the tuck rnd
- **4th tuck:** count 5 rounds down and work 5 rnds plain after the tuck rnd

5th tuck: K24, work tuck over the next 10 sts. Work 8 rnds even.
6th-9th tucks: Work 3 more tucks, spacing them as above.

Next rnd: Knit, placing marker after every 29th st. Knit around, working k2tog before each marker, and continuing around until 8 sts rem.

FINISHING
Run the tail of yarn through rem sts twice, then tighten to fasten off. Weave in ends. Turn the hat right side out so the purl side is showing.

Very British [DESIGNED BY STEFANIE THOMAS]

LEVEL OF DIFFICULTY

 Intermediate

SIZE

Circumference 21¼-22 in / 54-56 cm

MATERIALS

Yarn: (CYCA #5), Lana Grossa Royal Tweed (100% Merino; 110 yd/101 m / 50 g), Turquoise Heather 061, 100 g

Needles: U.S. size 7 / 4.5 mm: set of 5 dpn or 24 in / 60 cm circular

Pins

Sewing needle

Stiff felt or plastic film, 8 in x 4 in / 20 cm x 10 cm

GAUGE

18 sts and 30 rows in Cable Pattern = 4 x 4 in / 10 x 10 cm.

14 sts and 30 rows in St st = 4 x 4 in / 10 x 10 cm.

Adjust needle size to obtain correct gauge if necessary.

TEMPLATE

Page 90

CHART

Cable Pattern

Work as charted. Only odd-numbered rows are shown. On even-numbered rows, knit the knits and purl the purls. Work the 12-stitch repeat 8 times around the hat. Work Rnds 1-18 once, then Rnds 9-18 once, then Rnds 19-22 once.

Repeat = 12 sts

⊟ = purl

■ = knit

■■▱■■ = sl 2 to cn and hold in back, k2, k2 from cn

PATTERN STITCHES

Ribbing

All rnds: (K2, p2) around.

Stockinette Stitch (St st)

All rnds: Knit.

INSTRUCTIONS

CO 96 sts. Join to work in the rnd, being careful not to twist sts. Work 30 rnds in ribbing.

Work 32 rnds in Cable Pattern.

Next rnd: Work Cable Pattern and p2tog in each column between cables—80 sts rem.

Work 1 rnd even in pattern as set.

Change to St st.

Next rnd: (K2tog, k1) continuously around until 53 sts rem.

Next rnd: K2tog, knit to end of round—52 sts rem.

Work 6 rnds even.

Next rnd: K2tog around—26 sts.

Knit 4 rnds even.

FINISHING

Run the tail of yarn through rem sts and tighten to fasten off. Weave in ends.

Trace the template on page 90 onto the felt or plastic and cut out the brim insert. Fold the ribbing section to the outside. Insert the brim insert at the center front and hold in place with pins. Sew through both layers of the ribbing above the brim insert to shape the brim and hold the insert in place.

Chocolate Dream [DESIGNED BY EWA JOSTES]

LEVEL OF DIFFICULTY

 Intermediate

SIZE

Circumference 23¾ in / 60 cm

MATERIALS

Yarn: (CYCA #4), Schoppel-Wolle Reggae (100% wool; 110 yd/101 m / 50 g), Chocolate Dream 1993, 100 g

Needles: U.S. size 7 / 4.5 mm: 24-32 in / 60-80 cm

GAUGE

18 sts and 38 rows in garter stitch = 4 x 4 in / 10 x 10 cm.

Adjust needle size to obtain correct gauge if necessary.

PATTERN STITCHES

Garter Stitch

All rows: Knit.

Double Stitch

(for short rows)

Pull the first working yarn tightly to the back over the top of the needle so the first stitch of the needle is stretched taut, creating two stitches (one made from each leg of the stitch). When you come to this double-stitch on the next row, knit both strands together as 1 stitch.

INSTRUCTIONS

CO 40 sts, leaving a long tail to gather the top of the hat later.

Rows 1-4: Knit.

Row 5: Knit to the last st, do not knit the last st, turn.

Row 6: Work a double stitch, knit to the end of the row, turn.

Row 7: Knit to the double stitch, turn.

Rows 8-14: Repeat Rows 6 and 7 another 3 times, then repeat Row 6 once more.

Row 15: Knit to 2 sts before the double stitch, turn—33 sts.

Row 16: Work a double stitch, knit to the end of the row, turn.

Rows 17-28: Repeat Rows 15 and 16 another 7 times—12 double sts on ndl.

Row 29: Knit all sts, working each double stitch as 1 st—40 sts.

Repeat Rows 1-29 another 5 times. BO loosely. Sew CO and BO edges together.

FINISHING

Using the CO tail, weave the yarn through the 12 sts at the center top of the hat and tighten. Weave in ends.

Coolness [DESIGNED BY SUSANNA BRÜHL]

LEVEL OF DIFFICULTY

 Easy

SIZE

Circumference 20½-22 in / 52-56 cm

MATERIALS

Yarn: (CYCA #3), Schachenmayr/SMC Cotton Bamboo (50% cotton, 50% bamboo; 131 yd/120 m / 50 g), Violet 49, Graphite 98, 100 g each

(CYCA #3), Schachenmayr/SMC Catania (100% cotton; 136 yd/125 m / 50 g), Jade 253, 100 g

Needles: U.S. size 6 / 4 mm: set of 5 dpn, 8 in / 20 cm long

GAUGE

19 sts and 31 rows in St st with doubled yarn = 4 x 4 in / 10 x 10 cm.

Adjust needle size to obtain correct gauge if necessary.

PATTERN STITCHES

Brim
All rnds: (K3, p1) around.

Ribbing
All rnds: (K10, p2) around.

Note: This hat is worked throughout with a double strand of yarn.

INSTRUCTIONS

With 2 strands of Graphite held tog, CO 96 sts. Divide sts on 4 dpn and join to work in the rnd, being careful not to twist sts.
Work 13 rnds in Brim pattern. Change to Violet and work 4 rnds in Brim pattern.

Turn the knitting inside out. Knit 2 rounds to form a turning ridge for the brim.
Work 25 rnds in ribbing.
With Jade, work 13 rnds in ribbing.
In Graphite, work 6 rnds in ribbing.

CROWN DECREASES

Redistribute the sts on each of the 4 ndls as foll: P1, k10, p2, k10, p1 on each dpn.
Dec rnd 1: *P2tog, k8, p2tog twice, k8, p2tog; rep from * 3 more times—80 sts.
Work 1 rnd in pattern as est.
Dec rnd 2: *P2tog, k6, p2tog twice, k6, p2tog; rep from * 3 more times.
Rep last 2 rnds, with 2 fewer sts between p2tog decreases until 8 sts rem.

FINISHING

Run the tail of yarn through rem sts and tighten to fasten off. Weave in ends.

Tips: It is easier to work with a double strand of yarn if you wind the two strands together into a new ball. A stitch marker helps keep track of counting rounds, or you may use a loop of yarn to create your own marker.

Forget-me-not [DESIGNED BY URSULA AND MELANIE MARXER]

LEVEL OF DIFFICULTY
 Intermediate

SIZE
Circumference 20½-21¾ in / 52-55 cm

MATERIALS
Yarn: (CYCA #6), Lana Grossa Ragazza Everybody (80% Merino, 20% polyamide; 82 yd/75 m / 100 g), Burgundy/Wine Red/Cherry 02, 150 g

Needles: U.S. size 15 / 10 mm

Crochet hook, U.S. size N/P-15 / 10 mm

GAUGE
10 sts and 15 rows in St st = 4 x 4 in / 10 x 10 cm.

Adjust needle size to obtain correct gauge if necessary.

PATTERN STITCHES

K1, p1 Ribbing
All rows: (K1, p1) across.

K2, p2 ribbing
All rows: (K2, p2) across.

Stockinette Stitch (St st)
Row 1: Knit.
Row 2: Purl.
Rep rows 1-2 for pattern.

INSTRUCTIONS
CO 16 sts.

Work 1 row in K1, P1 ribbing.

Next row: M1 after each st—32 sts.

Work another 60 rows in K2, P2 ribbing.

Next row: (K2tog, p2tog) across.

Work 1 row in K1, P1 ribbing.

BO.

FINISHING
Fold the piece in half lengthwise, so the short ends are aligned. Sew one long edge together. Weave tail through the short ends of the strip; tighten and fasten off.

FLOWER
CO 5 sts. Work in St st until piece measures approx. 1 yd / 1 m long. Weave yarn through one long edge of the strip and tighten to form a blossom shape.

Bobble: With crochet hook, ch 1, work 5 dc in ch and gather tog. Sew bobble in center of flower. Sew flower on hat.

Weave in ends.

Spring Lights [DESIGNED BY SYLVIE RASCH]

LEVEL OF DIFFICULTY

 Experienced

SIZE

Circumference 20½-22¾ in / 52-58 cm

MATERIALS

Yarn: (CYCA #4), Schoppel Cashmere Queen (45% Merino, 35% cashmere, 20% silk; 153 yd/140 m / 50 g), Forest 6165, 50 g

Needles: U.S. sizes 4 and 10 / 3.5 and 6 mm: sets of 5 dpn

GAUGE

18 sts and 11 rows in St st on larger ndls = 4 x 4 in / 10 x 10 cm.

Adjust needle sizes to obtain correct gauge if necessary.

CHART

Star Pattern

Work all rnds as charted. Work the 12-st rep 8 times around the hat. Work Rnds 1-76 once.

INSTRUCTIONS

With smaller dpn, CO 96 sts; divide sts evenly onto 4 dpn. Join to work in the rnd, being careful not to twist sts. Work as charted, working first

■ = knit
− = purl
◣ = sl 1, k1, psso or ssk
◢ = k2tog
○ = yo
◆ = M1
▲ = sl 1, k2tog, psso
△ = M1R
◢ = M1L

= sl 1 to cn and hold in back, sl 1-kw-wyib, sl 1 from cn

= sl 1 to cn and hold in back, sl 1-kw-wyib, k1 from cn

= sl 1 to cn and hold in front, k1, sl 1-kw-wyib from cn

row of chart 12 times around for band. Change to larger dpn and work Rows 13-76 as charted—2 sts rem on each ndl.

FINISHING

Run the tail of yarn through rem sts and tighten to fasten off. Weave in ends.

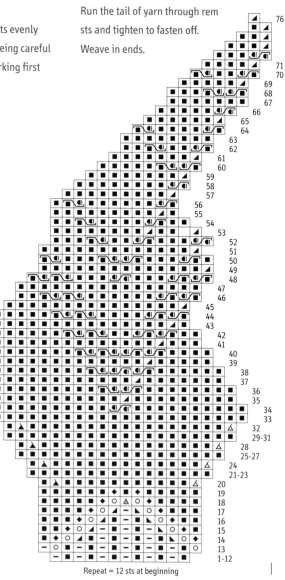

Repeat = 12 sts at beginning

Spring Fever [DESIGNED BY SUSANNA BRÜHL]

LEVEL OF DIFFICULTY
 Easy

SIZE
Circumference 20½-22 in / 52-56 cm

MATERIALS
Yarn: (CYCA #2), Schöller and Stahl Limone (100% cotton; 136 yd/125 m / 50 g), Birch 111 and Turquoise 131, 100 g each; Azure 136, 50 g

Needles: U.S. size 6 / 4 mm: 24 in / 60 cm circular

GAUGE
20 sts and 28 rows in St st with doubled yarn = 4 x 4 in / 10 x 10 cm.

Adjust needle size to obtain correct gauge if necessary.

PATTERN STITCHES
Stockinette Stitch (St st)
All rnds: Knit.

Reverse Stockinette Stitch (rev St st)
All rnds: Purl.

Ribbing
All rnds: (K3, p1) around.

Note: This hat is worked with two strands of yarn held together. It is easier to work with a double strand of yarn if both yarns are wound together into one ball.

INSTRUCTIONS
With 2 strands of Turquoise held together, CO 96 sts. Join to work in the rnd, being careful not to twist sts. Pm to indicate beg of rnd.
Work 16 rnds in ribbing.
Turn cuff inside out. Work 23 rnds in St st. (Change to Azure (2 strands held together) and work 1 rnd in St st and 4 rnds in rev St st, then change to Birch (hold 2 strands together) and work 16 rnds in St st) twice.
Next rnd: Change to Azure (2 strands) and knit.
Work 2 rnds in rev St st.
Eyelet rnd: (P11, yo, p2tog) around.
Next rnd: Purl.

Change to Turquoise (2 strands) and work 3 rnds in St st.

On 113th rnd, work saw-tooth edge BO as foll: *transfer the last st worked back to the left ndl, CO 4, BO 12; rep from * until all sts are bound off—12 points.

FINISHING
Run the tail of yarn through rem sts and tighten to fasten off. Weave in ends.

Make 2 twisted cords or braids 24 in / 60 cm long. Weave the cords through the eyelets in opposite directions, so one cord is on the inside and the other cord is on the outside between holes. Tie the ends of the cords tog to form rings. Let the ends dangle or tuck them inside the hat.

Tip: This can be worn as a hat or as a scarf, depending on whether the cords are pulled tightly to gather the fabric in or left open to form a ring.

Dreaming of Flowers [DESIGNED BY SYLVIE RASCH]

LEVEL OF DIFFICULTY

 Experienced

SIZE

Circumference 21¼-23¾ in / 54-60 cm

MATERIALS

Yarn: (CYCA #3), Schachenmayr/SMC Alpaca Premium (100% alpaca; 109 yd/100 m / 50 g), Fuschia 135, 100 g

Needles: U.S. sizes 4 / 3.5 mm and 10 / 6 mm: sets of 5 dpn

GAUGE

18 sts and 24 rows in St st on larger needles = 4 x 4 in / 10 x 10 cm.

Adjust needle sizes to obtain correct gauge if necessary.

CHART

Blossom Pattern

From Rows 19-34, only the odd-numbered rows are shown on the chart. On even-numbered rows, knit the knits and yarnovers and purl the purls. In all other rnds, work as charted. The repeat is 10 sts to begin, worked 8 times around the hat. Work Rnds 1-71 once.

INSTRUCTIONS

With smaller ndls, CO 80 sts; divide sts evenly onto 4 dpn. Join to work in the rnd, being careful not to twist sts. Work Rnds 1-12 in ribbing as charted.

Change to larger ndls and work Rnds 13-71 of chart. After the last rnd is worked, 2 sts rem on each ndl.

FINISHING

Run the tail of yarn through rem sts and tighten to fasten off. Weave in ends.

■ = knit
− = purl
O = yarnover
◣ = sl 1, k1, psso or ssk
◢ = k2tog
△ = sl 1, k2tog, psso
+ = M1
∩ = sl 2tog-kw, k1, p2sso

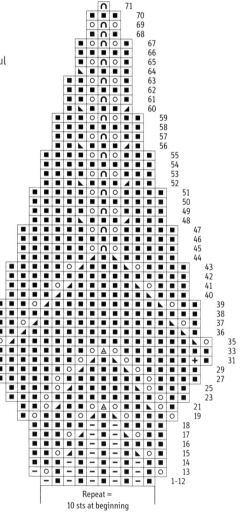

Repeat =
10 sts at beginning

Small Checks [DESIGNED BY EWA JOSTES]

LEVEL OF DIFFICULTY

 Intermediate

SIZE

Circumference 22½ in / 57 cm

MATERIALS

Yarn: (CYCA #1), Schoppel-Wolle Admiral (459 yd /420 m / 100 g), Natural 980, 100 g;

(CYCA #1), Schoppel-Wolle Crazy Zauberball (75% wool, 25% nylon; 459 yd/420 m / 100 g), Spring Is Here! 2136, 100 g

Needles: U.S. size 1-2 / 2.5 mm: set of 5 dpn

GAUGE

1 square of 27 sts = 1½ in / 4 cm.

Adjust needle size to obtain correct gauge if necessary.

PATTERN STITCHES

Garter Stitch in the Round

Rnd 1: Knit around.

Rnd 2: Purl around.

Repeat these 2 rounds.

Square

The squares are worked back and forth. Always knit the first and last st for selvage.

Row 1: With Admiral, k12, k3tog, k12.

Row 2: With Crazy Zauberball, knit.

Row 3: With Crazy Zauberball, p11, k3tog, p11.

Row 4: With Admiral, knit.

Row 5: With Admiral, k10, k3tog, k10.

Row 6: With Crazy Zauberball, knit.

Row 7: With Crazy Zauberball, p9, k3tog, p9.

Continue in this fashion, alternating colors and knit and purl rows, and working 1 st fewer before and after the center k3tog decrease each time, as above. Fasten off when 1 st remains.

INSTRUCTIONS

Begin with a tail of yarn long enough to sew a seam later.

FIRST ROW OF SQUARES

Square 1: CO 27 sts and knit 1 square.

Square 2: Hold the finished square in your left hand, with the diagonal decrease line running from bottom right to top left, and the working needle in your right hand. With Admiral pick up and knit 12 sts along the left edge of the square—13 sts. Using the backward loop cast-on, CO 14—27 sts total. Work next square as for the first.

Create 8 more squares as for Square 2—10 squares total. Separate the yarns.

SECOND ROW OF SQUARES

To begin, with Admiral, pick up and knit 13 sts along the top edge of the first square in the first row. CO 14. Work next square.

Continue to add squares around the second row in this fashion until you have another 10 squares. Break yarn, leaving a long tail. Sew the back seam.

BRIM

On the bottom edge of the first row of squares, with Admiral, pick up and knit 14 sts from each square—140 sts total. Divide sts evenly on 4 dpn (35 sts per ndl), placing a marker after 11 sts in the center of each needle.

Work 8 rnds in Garter St. BO.

CROWN

With Admiral, pick up and knit 13 sts from each square—130 sts total. Divide sts onto 4 dpn so there are 2 squares on each of 2 ndls and 3 squares on each of 2 more ndls. Place marker after each group of 13 sts.

Continue as follows:

Rnd 1: With Admiral, knit.

Rnd 2: With Admiral, purl.

Rnds 3 & 4: With Crazy Zauberball, knit.

Rnds 5 & 6: With Admiral, rep Rnds 1 & 2.

Rnd 7: With Crazy Zauberball, knit around, working k2tog before each marker—120 sts.

Rnd 8: With Crazy Zauberball, knit.

Rep Rnds 1-8 another 4 times—90 sts rem.

(cont. p. 90)

Templates

Continue to dec as follows:

Rnd 1: With Admiral, knit.

Rnd 2: With Admiral, purl.

Rnd 3: With Crazy Zauberball, knit around, working k2tog before each marker.

Rnd 4: With Crazy Zauberball, knit.

Rep Rnds 1-4 another 4 times—50 sts rem. Continue as above, decreasing every other rnd until 10 sts rem.

FINISHING

Run the tail of yarn through rem sts and tighten to fasten off. Weave in ends.

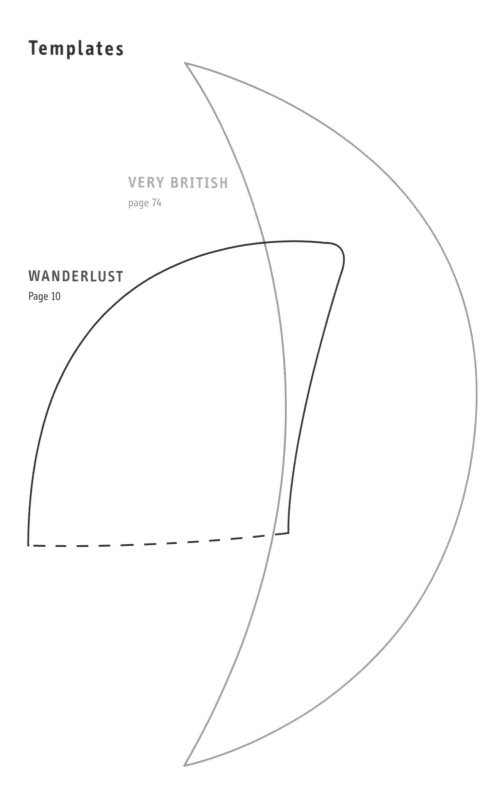

VERY BRITISH
page 74

WANDERLUST
Page 10

Charts

PURE NATURE

Page 8

- $\boxed{-}$ = purl
- $\boxed{\blacksquare}$ = knit
- $\boxed{\blacktriangle}$ = k2tog
- $\boxed{\blacktriangle}$ = sl 1, k1, psso or ssk
- $\boxed{\triangle}$ = p2tog
- $\boxed{\triangle}$ = sl 1 kw, k2tog, psso
- = sl 2 to cn and hold in front, k1, k2 from cn
- = sl 1 to cn and hold in back, k2, k1 from cn
- = sl 2 to cn and hold in front, p1, k2 from cn
- = sl 1 to cn and hold in back, k2, p1 from cn
- = sl 2 to cn and hold in back, k2, k2 from cn
- = sl 2 to cn and hold in front, k2, k2 from cn
- = sl 3 to cn and hold in back, k3, k3 from cn
- = sl 3 to cn and hold in front, k3, k3 from cn

WANDERLUST

Page 10

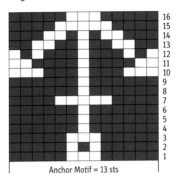

Anchor Motif = 13 sts

- $\square$ = K on RS, p on WS, then bring up a white bead to the knitting
- $\blacksquare$ = K on RS, p on WS

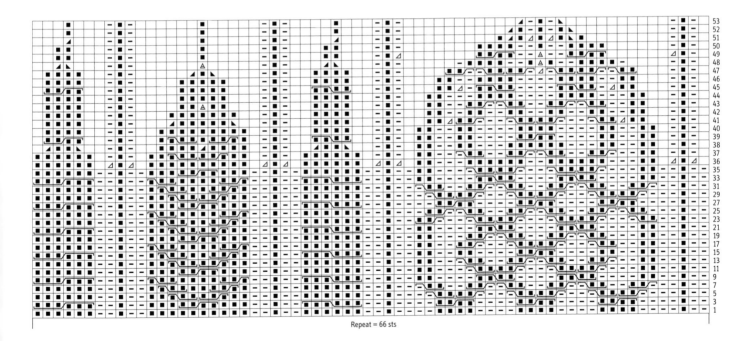

Repeat = 66 sts

UNDERSTATEMENT

Page 28

Note: Only odd-numbered rows shown on chart.

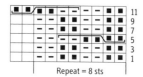

Repeat = 8 sts

$\boxed{-}$ = purl

$\boxed{\blacksquare}$ = knit

$\square$ = no stitch

= sl 2 to cn and hold in front, k2, p2, then k2 from cn

= sl 4 to cn and hold in back, k2, then p2, k2 from cn

MYSTERIOUS

Page 60

Note: Only odd-numbered rows shown on chart.

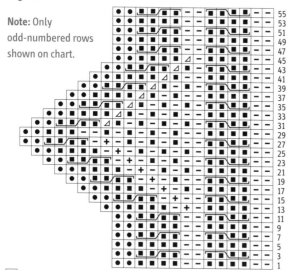

$\boxed{\blacksquare}$ = knit

$\boxed{-}$ = purl

$\boxed{\bullet}$ = selvage st

$\boxed{+}$ = M1

$\boxed{\triangle}$ = p2tog

= sl 2 to cn and hold in front, k2, k2 from cn

= sl 2 to cn and hold in back, k2, k2 from cn

FAR NORTH

Page 44

■ = knit with Navy Blue

■ = knit with Cherry

□ = knit with White

$\boxed{+}$ = M1

$\boxed{\blacktriangleleft}$ = k2tog

$\boxed{\blacktriangleleft}$ = sl 1, k1, psso or ssk

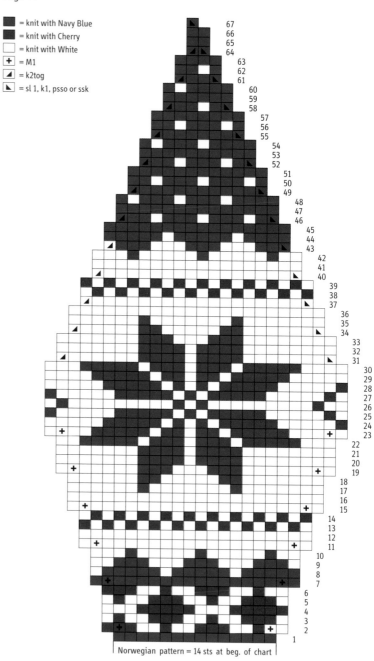

Norwegian pattern = 14 sts at beg. of chart

WINTER DREAM

Page 32

Star Pattern

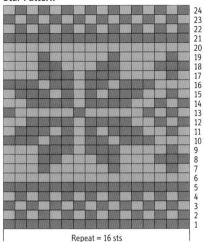

Repeat = 16 sts

Grid Pattern

Repeat =
2 sts

Dot Pattern

Repeat =
4 sts

= Light Gray Heather

= Janina Color

EITHER, OR

Page 54

Small Cable

Repeat = 11 sts

Large Cable

Repeat = 33 sts

 = purl

 = knit

 = sl 2 to cn and hold in back, k2, k2 from cn

 = sl 2 to cn and hold in front, k2, k2 from cn

 = sl 2 to cn and hold in front, p1, k2 from cn

 = sl 1 to cn and hold in back, k2, p1 from cn

 = sl 3 to cn and hold in back, k2, then p1, k2 from cn

 = sl 3 to cn and hold in front, k2, put the purl from the cn back onto the left needle and p1, k2 from cn

Argyle Motif

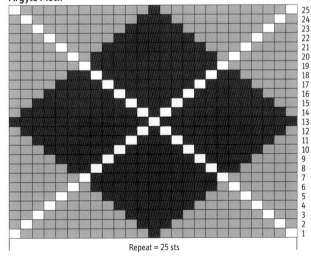

Repeat = 25 sts

 = Light Gray Heather

 = White

 = Black

Basic Techniques

Provisional Cast-On

A provisional cast-on allows you to work into the cast-on edge of a piece of knitting with no seam or pick-up ridge.

Crochet a loose chain with a contrasting color yarn. Work about 10 chains more than the number of stitches you need to cast on. Pick up and knit stitches in the back of the crochet chains. Be careful not to split the scrap yarn or it will be impossible to unravel the chain later without cutting it.

When removing the chain later, put the live stitches onto a knitting needle. You will have fewer stitches than you cast on because the edges do not form complete stitches. You can increase in the first row of knitting to add a missing stitch or two.

KNITTING WITH BEADS

Knit the stitch which will hold the bead, and slip it back onto the left needle. Put a bead on the bead needle and insert it onto the knitted stitch.

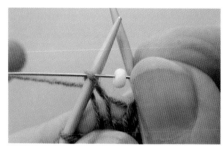

Pull the wire through the knitted stitch and through the bead.

Then use the wire to pull the knitted stitch through the bead.

Slip the beaded stitch onto the right needle.

If desired, you can leave the stitch on the right needle before adding the bead. You can also remove the stitch from the needles before adding the bead, but this makes it easy to drop a stitch.

KITCHENER STITCH

(Set-up) Hold the two pieces together on the two knitting needles, wrong sides together, positioned so the working strand comes from the first stitch on the front needle. Insert the tapestry needle into the first stitch on the back needle as if to knit, but don't take the stitch off its needle. Now insert the tapestry needle into the first stitch on the front needle as if to purl, and, again, don't take the stitch off the needle.

*(Back needle) Take the tapestry needle to the back needle and insert it in the first stitch as if to purl and remove that stitch from its needle.

Insert the tapestry needle into the next stitch as if to knit but do not remove it.

(Front needle) Take the tapestry needle to the front needle and insert it in the first stitch as if to knit and remove that stitch from its needle.

Insert the tapestry needle into the next stitch as if to purl but do not remove it.

Repeat steps from * until one stitch remains on each needle.

Follow the established pattern as well as possible with these two stitches. One st will be removed from its needle after the second pass of the tapestry needle; there will be no second stitch on that needle to go through before moving to the other needle. The final stitch will only be entered once with the tapestry needle. Fasten off.

POMPOMS

A pompom is a ball made out of many strands of wool tied together and trimmed into a round shape. To make a pompom, cut 2 circles out of stiff cardboard. The size of the circles should be about the same size as the finished pompoms. Make a hole in the center of each circle. The larger the hole is, the denser your pompom can be. Using a tapestry needle or a small ball of yarn, wrap the yarn around until the hole in the center is closed. The more wraps you make, the fuller your pompom will be. Cut the yarn. Insert the scissor tips between the two cardboard circles and cut the strands all the way around. Wrap a separate piece of yarn between the cardboard circles twice and knot securely. Remove the cardboard. Fluff the pompom and trim as desired. Pompoms can be sewn directly to a knitted garment or attached to a hanging cord or strand of yarn.

Abbreviations

approx.	approximately
BO	bind off (British—cast off)
CDD	centered double decrease
ch	chain
cn	cable needle
CO	cast on
cont	continue
dc	double crochet (British—treble crochet)
dec(s)	decrease(s)(ing)
dpn	double pointed needle(s)
inc(s)	increase(s)(ing)
k	knit
k2tog	knit 2 sts together
kf&b	knit into front and then back of same stitch
kw	knitwise (or as if to knit)
M1	make 1 increase (lift strand between 2 sts and knit into back loop)
M1L	make 1 left-leaning (see page 82)
M1p	make 1 purlwise
M1R	make 1 right-leaning (see page 82)
ndl(s)	needle(s)

p	purl
p2tog	purl 2 sts together
pm	place marker
pwise	purlwise (or as if to purl)
rem	remain(s)(ing)
rep	repeat
rnd(s)	round(s)
RS	right side
sc	single crochet (British—double crochet)
sl	slip
sl 1-k1-psso	slip 1 k1, knit 1, pass the slipped st over
sl 2-k1-p2sso	slip 2 sts tog (as if to k2tog), knit 1, pass the 2 slipped sts over
ssk	(slip 1 kw) twice, insert left needle into front of the 2 sts just slipped and k2tog-tbl
st(s)	stitch(es)
tog	together
WS	wrong side
wyib	with yarn in back
wyif	with yarn in front
yo	yarnover

Yarn Information

Webs – America's Yarn Store
75 Service Center Road
Northampton, MA 01060
800-367-9327
www.yarn.com
customerservice@yarn.com

Westminster Fibers (US)
8 Shelter Drive
Greer, SC 29650
800-445-9276
info@westminsterfibers.com
www.westminsterfibers.com

(in Canada)
10 Roybridge Gate, Suite 200
Vaughan, ON L4H 3M8
800-263-2354

If you are unable to obtain any of the yarns used in this book, they can be replaced with yarns of a similar weight and composition. Please note, however, the finished hats may vary slightly from those shown, depending on the yarn used.

For more information on selecting or substituting yarn contact your local yarn shop or an online store, they are familiar with all types of yarns and would be happy to help you. Additionally, the online knitting community at *Ravelry.com* has forums where you can post questions about specific yarns. Yarns come and go so quickly these days and there are so many beautiful yarns available.